ADVANCED BASIC
Data Structures and File Techniques

Roy A. Boggs
Department of Computer Systems
The University of Toledo

RESTON PUBLISHING COMPANY, INC.
A Prentice-Hall Company
Reston, Virginia

Library of Congress Cataloging in Publication Data

Boggs, Roy A.
  Advanced BASIC.

  Includes index.
  1.. Basic (Computer program language)   2. Data
structures (Computer science)   3. File organization
(Computer science)   I. Title.   II. Title: Advanced
B.A.S.I.C.
QA76.73.B3B63   1983   001.64'24   83-11144
ISBN 0-8359-0163-7
ISBN 0-8359-0161-0 (pbk.)

©1984 by
Reston Publishing Company, Inc.
A Prentice-Hall Company
Reston, Virginia 22090

The final typesetting was done on a TyXSET 1000 in Reston,
Virginia, using a Mergenthaler Omnitech/2100. The galleys and
page makeup were also done on the TyXSET 1000 system using a
Canon LBP-10 Laser Printer for page proofs.

TyXSET 1000 is a trademark of TyX Corporation.

10   9   8   7   6   5   4   3   2   1

Printed in the United States of America.

Contents

Preface

BASIC, by its very name,

Beginner's **A**ll-purpose **S**ymbolic **I**nstruction **C**ode

has long been considered a good language for students to learn in a
beginning computer course. But the name is misleading. Not only
is BASIC an easy language to learn, but also it has become a powerful, extremely versatile, high-level computer language. Where once
BASIC was limited to the classroom, we now find it used to write
complicated operating systems. Many businesses and consulting
firms code only in BASIC; and it has become common practice for
professional programmers to use BASIC for their own programs,
while using other languages where required.

ADVANCED BASIC is primarily concerned with data
management and applications development. As soon as BASIC

programming goes beyond games and single program applications, the programmer is faced with analyzing, collecting, coding, storing, retrieving, and updating data. An understanding of data structures and file techniques is the next logical step in learning to design and develop applications using BASIC.

BASIC owes much of its popularity and growth to a rapid transition over the last several years. The earliest versions contained only simple program control statements, such as GOTO, IF-THEN, and FOR-NEXT. These early versions were usually limited to numeric library functions [TAN(X), INT(X), etc.], numeric tables and arrays [DIM A(5)], and user-defined functions. This rather small set of statements was sufficient, however, for students to prepare and execute some rather complicated routines, while at the same time providing an introduction to computing.

The next general development, EXTENDED BASIC, added string features [DIM A$(12)], some useful branching statements [ON..GOTO, IF..THEN/ELSE], and extended output controls [TAB(X), PRINT USING]. Together with the above statements, these are treated in textbooks introducing BASIC. They comprise a set of instructions that can be referred to as STANDARD BASIC. The first two chapters contain a brief review of this set, and a knowledge of STANDARD BASIC is then assumed for the following chapters.

There exist today, however, versions of BASIC that go far beyond STANDARD BASIC. An example can be found in BASIC-PLUS, where string manipulation features, extended variable names, additional library string functions, and file management routines are common features. BASIC-PLUS-2 * has gone a step further by extending variable names to match those of any other high-level language, and by providing the full range of I/O and file maintenance features found in even the most developed computer language.

At the same time, BASIC has retained its ease of use and its uncomplicated syntax. It enjoys status as the most preferred language on micros and minis, even where data and information systems have been implemented. This much extended set of instructions is referred to here as ADVANCED BASIC. It represents an extension over the BASIC instructions found in current texts, which remain limited regardless of specialized titles and examples.

* VAX-11 BASIC and BASIC-PLUS-2 are trademarks of Digital Equipment Corporation. Other versions of BASIC are used where significant functions might not be otherwise exemplified.

This text introduces more advanced data structures and file techniques. In an attempt to avoid an author's self-developed code with little or no applicability, VAX-11 BASIC is often used throughout the text to illustrate examples. This version of BASIC was selected because it represents the most developed version available to college students. Examples written in VAX-11 BASIC form a pseudocode that is quickly and easily understood. It is, therefore, not necessary for the student to transpose logic structures into program routines. Any application written in this version of BASIC can be easily rewritten in another version of BASIC. This text can, therefore, be used with almost any operating system supporting a BASIC capable of file manipulation.

On the computer systems of major vendors, BASIC runs in both interactive and batch modes. Where earlier versions were almost entirely interactive and/or time-shared, current versions of BASIC can easily be used to generate object modules for production job streams as well as any application where stored programs are run over and over.

There are, to be sure, still versions of BASIC available that are completely interactive and that are designed solely for time-sharing services. But these versions are becoming fewer in number. For the present, micros remain single-user systems; and core storage on the more powerful models (48k and up) hardly notices the different versions of BASIC. On the minis, where today core memory is easily between 1 and 4 megabytes, compiler-driven versions producing object modules are running as fast and as efficiently as are interactive versions. This feature of BASIC has expanded its range of applications to include all forms of data information processing.

One current trend, however, that should perhaps not be so quickly applied to current versions of BASIC is that of structuring everything. The disturbing aspect of "structured" BASIC with DOWHILE and SET FLAG statements is that the pseudocode usually becomes so convoluted that it destroys BASIC's main virtue, its simplicity. Obviously programs should be written as clearly as possible, be modularized, and be well documented. But standardized BASIC statements (such as FOR..NEXT, GOSUB..RETURN, REM), when properly used, and when coupled with good variable names, offer perhaps the clearest approach to programming among the high-level languages.

A claim is made here that applications written in BASIC can be developed more quickly and maintained without loss of capabilities and with less expense than other high-level languages. This is important. A great many people have been introduced to problem solving using standard BASIC because BASIC has continued to be easy to learn, easy to write, and readily available on a wide range of systems. Almost every college student majoring in a scientific or a business subject has been introduced to BASIC, and the number of junior high and high school students who know BASIC is growing every day. BASIC's extended features now make it an excellent language for managing data and information systems. This is not hypothesizing about what might be, or about what might be best. Extended versions of BASIC exist, and a large number of people have been introduced to them.

The material in this text is intended as an introduction to the second level of programming. It is an introduction to data structures and file techniques, using BASIC to illustrate examples. These examples are, in turn, used to illustrate programming solutions encountered in designing data and information systems. The material is specific in delineation, while examples are, by necessity, kept general. It is hoped that this introduction will offer students an opportunity to expand their programming capabilities, while at the same time demonstrating some of the the possibilities of using BASIC as an application language.

Roy A. Boggs

Standard BASIC

The material presented in this and the next chapter is intended primarily as a review of those BASIC statements most commonly found in introductory texts. Some texts may contain a few more or a few less of these statements, but when taken together, they form a common starting point called Standard BASIC.

The set of statements in these two chapters was taken from a survey of current beginning texts, as well as from introductory texts for data processing containing a module or chapter on BASIC. Standard BASIC, therefore, does not represent some logical or pedagogical grouping. Rather, it is a starting point with which a large number of students should be familiar.

In fact, three peculiar aspects emerge upon examination of Standard BASIC statements. One is the usual inclusion of almost all of the numeric library functions and, conversely, the exclusion of almost all of the large number of string library functions. This remains true even in those beginning texts whose titles advertise a special interest in business and/or data processing. A second aspect which emerges in the most elementary of texts is the variety of MATRIX statements discussed. Exactly when and why all of these are to be used is confusing to all but a handful of beginners. These statements are, therefore, quite often skimmed or ignored in beginning courses. And the third aspect is the often rather loose regard for text formatting statements. TAB and PRINT USING are either ignored or else quickly presented, without pause for sufficient and useful examples.

There are, of course, historical trails behind the format of current Standard BASIC texts. What began as a set of useful instructions has quickly become a sophisticated high-level language. The result is often a rather loose set of statements and rules for writing guessing games and completing some forms of classroom assignments. Much is left to be learned for actual applications programming.

It will be assumed throughout this text that the material in this and the next chapter has at some time been reviewed. Chapter I presents a review of the more general BASIC statements. They will be familiar to most students. Perhaps the only exception will be the various PRINT formats which should be examined carefully.

Chapter II will examine arrays and functions. Although not included in most beginning BASIC texts, string functions will be introduced in this chapter. They are included with numeric functions for completeness of presentation and for purposes of comparison. This is an important chapter. A working knowledge of arrays will then be assumed in all of the following chapters.

For the other statements in these two chapters, it will not be necessary to actually have studied each one in detail. A general knowledge will probably be sufficient. This material is intended as a common starting point, and is not meant to exhaust all possible features of Standard BASIC. Details and further examples may be found in most introductory texts.

I.A VARIABLE NAMES

In computer programming, a variable name is a character or a group of characters referring to a given value. Values may be changed during the execution of a program, while the variable names themselves remain the same. In general, variable names must begin with a letter of the alphabet, A–Z. Depending upon the version of BASIC being used, they may be from 1 to 29 characters in length. Whereas earlier versions of BASIC restricted variable names to a single alphabetic character and/or a number, this is no longer the case. On some smaller systems, however, only the first three characters are significant; i.e., confusion can result when two different variables begin with the same three characters.

I.A.1 Numeric Variables

Numeric variable names begin with an alphabetic character (A–Z) and can be from 1 to 29 characters in length. Under no condition can a letter of the alphabet or a special character (except the decimal point) become the value of a numeric variable.

Variable names should also be designed to be as meaningful as possible. In longer programs containing many variable names, it can become almost impossible to remember one from another. Whereas earlier versions of BASIC restricted variable names to one letter and one number (A1), it is now possible to create more expressive names. A little thought in the beginning will save a lot of work when the program needs checking for errors.

Possible numeric variables:

CORRECT VARIABLE	WARNING
A	Not meaningful.
Z15	Not meaningful.
DOLLARS	Might be confused with DOLLS, DOLOMITE, etc., on some systems.
NEW_BALANCE	"_" as a special character is not allowed on some systems. Never use the minus sign " – ".

LET BALANCE = 12.95

I.A.2 String Variables

A string numeric variable holds string data, including numbers. A string variable also begins with an alphabetic character and can be from 1 to 29 characters in length. However, string variables must end with a dollar sign ($).

While string variables may contain numbers ("234 PINE STREET"), they may not be used in mathematical equations.

String variable names should also be as meaingful as possible. Possible string variables:

CORRECT VARIABLE	WARNING
A$	Not meaningful.
Z15$	Not meaningful.
BOARD$	Might be confused with BOAR$, BOAT$, etc., on some systems
BOOK_TITLE$	"_" is a special character.
DATA$	Might be a reserved word. Better DA.TA$

LET NAME$ = "Susan B. Anthony"

In most versions of BASIC, values assigned to string variables must be enclosed within quotation marks. Whereas numbers are always found between blank spaces, string variables may contain blank spaces. BASIC needs the quotes to know where a string is supposed to begin and end.

I.B OPERATORS AND RELATIONS

I.B.1 Mathematical Operations: $+, -, *, /, \wedge$

The operational symbols found in BASIC are similar to those used in ordinary mathematics. A mathematical value is *first* determined for the expression to the right of the equal sign, and the resulting value is *assigned to a single variable* to the left of the equal sign.

Addition	+	$A = B + C$
Subtraction	−	$A = B - C$
Muliplication	*	$A = B * C$
Division	/	$A = B / C$
Exponentiation	$\wedge$ (**)	$A = B \wedge C$

(Note that in some versions, two asterisks (**) are used instead of the vertical arrow ($\wedge$) for exponentiation.)

I.B.2 Operators and Hierarchical Groups

While the left side of an equation may consist of only a single variable, the right side may include as many variables as desired, and these may include as many operational symbols as necessary.

Within a group of variables, all operations will be performed from left to right—and all operations will be carried out in accordance with the following well-defined hierarchy:

1. Exponentiation $\wedge$
2. Multiplication *and* Division $* /$
3. Addition *and* Subtraction $+ -$

BASIC works from left to right within the equation. First, it raises all appropriate variables to their powers. Second, it goes back and performs all multiplications and/or divisions. And then it goes back again and performs all additions and/or subtractions.

$$A + B / C * D$$

$$16 = 4 + 8 / 2 * 3$$

In this example, B will be divided by C ($8/2 = 4$); then the result will be multiplied by D ($4*3 = 12$); and finally this result will be added to A ($4 + 12 = 16$).

In some instances, the natural hierarchy of operations does not match the mathematical operations to be performed. When this is the case, parentheses are included within the equation to denote the order of computation.

$$(A + B) / (C*D)$$

$$(4 + 8) / (2*3)$$

$$2 = 12 / 6$$

CONVENTIONAL	BASIC
$\dfrac{A}{B + E}$	A/(B + E)
$\sqrt{\dfrac{2DC}{C}}$	SQR(2*D*C/C)
$(1 + n)^m$	(1 + n)**m

When parentheses are present in an expression, the operators within the parentheses will be performed first, hierarchically from left to right. This is also true for nested parentheses, where the innermost parentheses will be performed first, the next innermost, and so on. Note that parentheses always come in pairs. Each left parenthesis must be accompanied by a right parenthesis. Failure to correctly match parentheses will cause either incorrect results or a syntax error.

I.B.3 Relations: $=, <>, <, <=, >, >=$

Relations are used to express conditions of equality and/or inequality. They are used as one would use them in mathematical expressions, except that double expressions are broken down into two symbols.

$=$	EQUAL TO
$<>$	NOT EQUAL TO
$>$	GREATER THAN
$>=$	GREATER THAN OR EQUAL TO
$<$	LESS THAN
$<=$	LESS THAN OR EQUAL TO

In most BASIC systems, the order of the double relation is fixed. For example, when using the "$<=$" relation, the "$<$" sign must come before the "$=$" sign.

CONVENTIONAL	BASIC
$A \neq B$	$A <> B$
$A \geq B$	$A >= B$
$A \leq B$	$A <= B$

I.C GENERAL STATEMENTS

I.C.1 REM

One of the most common tests of a good program is its documentation. For internal documentation—that is, documentation within the program itself—BASIC uses the REMark statement (REM). Each time a copy of the program is printed, the remark statements are also printed. They cause no operations to be performed by the computer.

```
ln  REM text

100 REM Calculate Square Roots

10 REM     ********************************
20 REM     *                              *
30 REM     *   This text introduces BASIC *
40 REM     *                              *
50 REM     ********************************
```

NOTE: In this and in the following, ln = line number. The BASIC verb is in capital letters; and the rest of the statement, if there is any, is given in small letters. At the least, each statement must begin with a line number and contain a verb.

Remark statements have no effect on program logic and are used solely to provide documentation. They thus have no effect on the running of the program, good or bad, and can be used to the advantage of the programmer and those who must subsequently perform maintenance on the program. *Good programs are well documented.*

I.C.2 LET

The LET statement is used to assign a value to a variable. The value on the right side is assigned to the left-hand variable.

ln LET variable = number, string, variable, or formula

100 LET A = (B + C) / 2

100 LET STRING$ = "ABCD"

Some versions of BASIC permit multiple assignments (100 LET A = B = C = D = 100). Other versions omit the verb LET (100 A = B = C = D = 100).

I.C.3 STOP, END

Both the STOP and END statements cause the program to terminate. They differ, however, in that the STOP statement can occur anywhere within the program, and the END statement is the last statement in the program.

ln STOP

ln END

A program may have multiple STOP statements, but only one END statement. A few versions of BASIC will not run unless the last statement is END. Others will run and terminate whenever a STOP is reached, even though there is no END statement.

I.C.4 Sample Program

```
100 REM    Sample program calculating
110 REM     monthly interest payments
120                                                      REM
200 PRINT "Enter amount, number years, rate ==> ";
210 INPUT AMOUNT, YEARS, RATE
220                                                      REM
300 LET PAYMENT = (AMOUNT * (12 * YEARS) * RATE) / 100
310                                                      REM
400 PRINT "Payment per month = ";PAYMENT
410 PRINT
420 PRINT "Another run (Y/N) = ";
430 INPUT ANS$
440 IF ANS$ = "Y" THEN 200
500                                                      REM
510 END
```

I.D PROGRAM CONTROL

I.D.1 Branching

I.D.1.a Unconditional: GOTO, ON..GOTO

GOTO provides for an unconditional transfer of the flow of the program to another statement in the program.

```
ln  GOTO n
```

```
100 GOTO 50
```

Here ln is the current statement number, and n is the number of the next statement to be executed. In the example, when the flow of the program reaches line 100, the next line of the program to be executed will be line 50.

Multiple transfers using single statements are also possible in BASIC. Based upon a numerical value, control of the program is transferred to one of several statements.

```
ln  ON formula GOTO n1,n2,n3...
```

```
100 ON K GOTO 200,300,400
```

```
100 ON (A+B) GOTO 200,300,400
```

When this statement is executed, control is passed to the line number corresponding to n1, n2, n3, etc., depending upon the value of the formula. If K = 1, go to line 200; if K = 2, go to line 300; or if K = 3, go to line 400. If A = 1 and B = 2, then the next statement would be line 400.

The number of lines that can be specified is usually limited to the number of line numbers that can be typed on one line. On some larger systems, several lines of numbers are possible. The same line number may occur more than once, but the line number must exist within the program.

```
100 ON K GOTO 50, 100, 50, 100
```

NOTE: If, in the above example, K does not have a value or 1, 2, 3, or 4, a fatal error may occur and the program terminate. It is always a good idea to check the value of the variable before using ON..GOTO.

I.D.1.b   Conditional: IF..THEN

In contrast to an unconditional branch in which transfer of program control is made each time a particular line is executed, the IF..THEN statement is used to make a transfer only if a certain condition is found to be *true*. Should the condition be false, transfer will not be made, and execution of the program will continue with the next line of the program.

```
ln  IF relationship THEN n
```

```
100 IF A>B THEN 500
110 LET...
     .
     .
     .
500 LET...
```

Statement number 500 will be executed next if A>B; otherwise statement number 110 will be performed next.

On most systems, transfer may be made to any line of the program except the IF..THEN statement itself. A few systems, however, do not permit transfer to a REM or other similar statements.

I.D.2   Loops: FOR(FOR..NEXT)NEXT

A loop is a sequence of consecutive statements whose execution is to be repeated a certain number of times. Loops can be constructed using branching statements but the FOR..NEXT statement generally provides an easier method for constructing loops. Use of this statement can also help make a program more legible because the beginning and end of the loop are easily recognizable.

The loop begins with the FOR..TO statement, and ends with a NEXT statement. All statements in between belong to the loop.

```
ln   FOR index = n1 TO n2 STEP n3
     .
     .
ln   NEXT index

100 FOR X = 1 TO 10 STEP 2
    .
    .
300 NEXT X

100 FOR KOUNT = 10 TO END_OF_KOUNT
    .
    .
300 NEXT KOUNT
```

Index begins with the value of n1 and will be incremented by the value of n3 until it is equal to or larger than n2.

In the first example, X will have the initial value of 1. It will be increased by a step of 2 each time the program reaches line 300 and goes back to line 100. This will continue until the value of X is equal to or greater than 10. In this case, 1, 3, 5, 7, and 9, or a total of five loops, will be performed.

In the second example, KOUNT will have the initial value of 10. It will be increased by 1 until it equals the value of END_OF_KOUNT. An increment of 1 is assumed as a default if STEP n3 is omitted.

The STEP feature, when used, may be positive, negative, an integer, or a fraction.

It is also possible to transfer out of a loop, using the IF..THEN statement.

```
100 FOR X = 1 TO 15
    .
    .
200      IF X>Y THEN 500
    .
    .
300 NEXT X
    .
    .
500 LET. .
```

Loops may also be nested if certain rules are followed. Nested loops may not overlap. One loop must be completely contained within the other. Also, a different index must be used for each loop in a nest. To do otherwise would be confusing.

```
    ┌──►100 FOR X = 1 TO 25
    │        .
    │        .
    │  ┌─►200       FOR Y = 1 TO 10
    │  │     .
    │  │     .
    │  └─►300       NEXT Y
    │        .
    │        .
    └──►400 NEXT X
```

Most versions of BASIC will not permit transfer to a statement within a loop; rather the FOR statement must be the first statement to be referenced. Each FOR statement must also have a corresponding NEXT statement. And in some versions, it is possible to omit the index. For purposes of clarity, however, it is usually best kept as part of NEXT statement.

I.D.3 Sample Program

```
10 REM Example of a nested loop
20                                                            REM
30 FOR X = 1 TO 4
40      FOR Y = 1 TO 4
50           PRINT X * Y,
60      NEXT Y
70 PRINT
80 NEXT X
90                                                            REM
100 END
```

Result:

1	2	3	4
2	4	6	8
3	6	9	12
4	8	12	16

I.D.4   Subroutines: GOSUB/RETURN, ON..GOSUB

The purpose of writing subroutines is to set aside a block of statements which would otherwise be repeated at different places throughout the program. Subroutines are also used to break longer programs into well-modularized segments for ease of program development and maintenance. The various modules are then fitted together to form a single program.

In BASIC, subroutines do not have names. They are referenced by line numbers and continue to a RETURN statement.

```
ln  GOSUB n
        .
        .
        .
ln  RETURN
```

```
   ┌──50  GOSUB 200
   │ ►60   .
   │  70   .
   │◄─100 GOSUB 200
   │ ►110    .
   │         .
   │         .
   └─►200 REM SUBROUTINE
   │         .
   └───300 RETURN
```

Note that the flow of the program goes from the GOSUB n statement to the appropriate line, here line 200; the RETURN, however, is to the line following the GOSUB statement, here line 60 or line 110.

Subroutines may also be nested, but they may not overlap. And in BASIC, subroutines do not use arguments.

Two additional GOSUB statements are also found in BASIC.

```
ln IF relationship THEN GOSUB n
```

and

```
ln ON formula GOSUB n1,n2,n3...
```

These statements follow the conventions of both the IF and the ON statements. Their use greatly increases programming flexibility and efficiency. They should be considered whenever complex and/or large programs are being written.

I.D.5 Sample Program

```
100 REM     Sample program calculating
110 REM      monthly interest payments
120                                                          REM
200 PRINT "Enter amount, number years, rate = ";
210 INPUT AMOUNT, YEARS, RATE
220                                                          REM
300 GOSUB 520
310                                                          REM
400 PRINT "Payment per month = ";PAYMENT
410 PRINT
420 PRINT "Another run (Y/N) = ";
430 INPUT ANS$
440 IF ANS$ = "Y" THEN 200
450 STOP
460                                                          REM
500 REM   Subroutine to calculate interest
510                                                          REM
520 LET PAYMENT = (AMOUNT * (12 * YEARS) * RATE) / 100
530 RETURN
540                                                          REM
600 END
```

I.E DATA INPUT

In data and information systems, data exist as entities, along with the program. They are communicated to and from the program by means of input and output (I/O) statements. Since most run-time errors are caused by incorrect data management, the material in this and the following paragraphs, as well as the following chapters, is extremely important. It is true that if you put garbage in, you will get garbage out [GIGO]; but many systems fail to work because at some point programmers make garbage out of good data [GOGD]. It is only through a solid understanding of input and output processes that an application can be properly designed.

I.E.1 Data

In BASIC, data may be included within the program itself. When this happens, the data cannot be changed from one run to another unless a program statement, the DATA statement, is rewritten. These data are *compile-time* data because once a program is compiled, they stay the same. An example of compile-time data would be a static array whose contents rarely, if ever, change.

Data may also exist outside of the program. These are *execution-time* data and are entered as the program is being executed. These data exist independently of the program. Programs need not be recompiled each time the data changes. Such data are also called *interactive* data.

I.E.1.a Compile-Time: READ/DATA/RESTORE

When the READ and DATA statements are used, data are provided as part of the program.

```
ln  READ list
    .
    .
ln  DATA values

100 READ    NAMES$, GRADE
    .
    .
900 DATA JONES, 92
910 DATA SMITH, 87

10   REM        STUDENT TEST AVERAGES
20                                              REM
30   READ NAME$, TEST1, TEST2, TEST3
35     IF NAME$ = "END" THEN 100
40                                              REM
50   PRINT \ PRINT
60   PRINT NAME$,  (TEST1 + TEST2 + TEST3) / 3
70                                              REM
80   DATA Dave Smith, 90, 94, 88
82   DATA Rita Jones, 100, 79, 82
84   DATA Kay Makey, 88, 93, 76
85   DATA END, 0, 0, 0
90                                              REM
100 END
```

Result:

Dave Smith	90.6666
Rita Jones	87
Kay Makey	85.6666

Each time a READ statement is executed, values are assigned to corresponding variables in the list. Values and variable types must match, strings to strings and numbers to numbers. Note that both variables and values are separated by commas. If strings are to include commas, colons, or leading blanks, they must be enclosed in quotes.

```
900 DATA "Today's quote: 'walk, run, race'."
```

DATA statements may appear anywhere in the program. Sometimes they occur along with the READ statement, but usually they are grouped together at the end of the program. In either case, they will be read in the order in which they occur in the program.

The RESTORE statement is used to read the data more than once.

```
ln RESTORE
```

Each time the program reaches a RESTORE statement, it returns to the first data value of the first DATA statement and continues processing from that point. The RESTORE statement is quite often used in processing blocks of data forming a table. Each READ searches for a data item; then the data is RESTOREd for the next search.

I.E.1.b   Interactive: INPUT, LINPUT

When an INPUT statement is encountered during the execution of a program, execution stops and a question mark (?) appears on the terminal. The user must then respond with a number or string value which is assigned to the variable in the INPUT list. Execution then begins with the next line of the program.

```
ln   INPUT list

100 INPUT NAME$, GRADE

100 INPUT "ENTER NAME, GRADE"; NAME$, GRADE
```

Data items are separated by commas, and they must match in type the corresponding variables in the list. A string value cannot be entered for a numeric variable. Also, all data requested by the INPUT statement must be entered, separated by commas, before execution of the program can continue.

I.E.2   Sample Program

```
10 REM   Student grades averages
20                                                          REM
30 PRINT "Enter name [END], grade, grade, grade = = > ";
32 INPUT NAME$, TEST1, TEST2, TEST3
35      IF NAME$ = "END" THEN 90
40                                                          REM
50 PRINT NAME$, (TEST1 + TEST2 + TEST3) / 100
60 PRINT
70 GOTO 30
80                                                          REM
90 END
```

LINPUT is used to enter strings and to assign all characters except the line terminator (carriage-return) to a string variable.

```
ln  LINPUT string
```

```
100 LINPUT "ENTER TEXT"; LINE$
```

An example on a terminal would look like this:

```
ENTER TEXT? "Charles, come here!" <CR>
```

with the result that LINE$ is assigned the value: "Charles, come here!" (complete with quotes). LINPUT treats the string value it accepts from the terminal as a string of data.

In some versions of BASIC, a distinction is made between the semicolon (;) and the comma(,) at the end of an input statement. The semicolon results in a question mark appearing on the terminal; and the comma shifts to the next tab. Both then await input and/or a carriage return.

On some systems, INPUT LINE is used to enter strings. Sometimes comment strings (i.e., "ENTER TEXT") are not permitted.

```
ln  INPUT LINE string
```

```
100 INPUT LINE TEXT$
```

I.F   DATA OUTPUT: PRINT

Data is sent to the various output devices via the PRINT command. A single PRINT statement followed by a variable prints a single line containing the value of the variable.

```
ln  PRINT list

100 A$ = "I want to go home. "
110 PRINT A$

100 PRINT "I want to go home. "

100 INTEREST = PRINCIPAL * INTEREST_RATE
110 PRINT INTEREST

100 PRINT (PRINCIPAL * INTEREST_RATE)
```

In each of these examples, the value of the variable or string following the PRINT will be printed, followed by a carriage-return and a line-feed. When running interactively, output is defaulted to the terminal. In batch, output is sent to the line printer.

I.F.1   Line Formats

BASIC assumes the output default device to be a terminal. "Default" means that, unless otherwise specified, the maximum number of columns per page will be somewhere between 72 and 80. This setting is convenient and permits programs to be run on a wide variety of terminals and line-printers. More options for both types of devices will be found in the following chapters. There exists among the many versions of BASIC a wide variety of output options that permit output on devices from pocket computers to high-resolution laser printers, including the entire spectrum of colors. The following examples are considered general in nature and are intended as an introduction. Reference can then be made to texts and manuals for more sophisticated routines.

I.F.1.a   Semicolon   (MARGIN)

Semicolons are used to separate items in a list. Each positive value in the list will be printed with a leading blank. If the value is negative, the leading blank is replaced with the minus sign. Extra spaces between items are treated as strings and enclosed in quotes.

```
100 PRINT 5; 10; 15; − 20; "  "; 25

          5    10    15  -20      25

100  LET A$ = "JANE"
110  PRINT "The answer is "; A$; ". "

          The answer is JANE.
```

Note the single space between the 15 and the minus sign, and the four spaces between −20 and 25. In the second example, note the space between "is" and the ending quote. This space is necessary so that A$ will appear after the word "is", but with an intervening space.

If the number of characters sent to the output device is more than 72 (80), the first 72 (80) characters will be printed on the current line, and the remaining characters will then be printed on the following line(s). When using a terminal, it is, therefore, a good idea to limit output to 72 (80) characters or less.

For hard-copy devices, such as line printers, a few versions of BASIC have a command to override the default and permit up to 132 characters per line. The command is usually MARGIN, or a similar word.

```
ln  MARGIN n

100 MARGIN 132
```

If MARGIN is not followed by a number, the margins are usually not reset. This statement needs only to be given once. It must, however, be given before a PRINT statement is used if the margins are to be changed for that PRINT statement. A good idea is to put this statement in the first several lines of the program.

I.F.1.b Comma

When commas are used instead of semicolons, the output is tabulated; i.e., it is put automatically into columns.

```
100 PRINT 5,10,15,20,25,30

    5   10   15   20
   25   30
```

When a comma is placed between items in a list, it controls the location of the output much the same as preset tabs on a typewriter. In BASIC, this is usually a spacing of 16 columns; and up to four columns are available per line. The terminal screen is considered to have four "zones" per line, with each zone 16 spaces in width. In the example above, up to four numbers will be printed per line. (On line-printers, the MARGIN statement can be used to reset the number of columns beyond the four zones.)

If, as in the above example, there are more than four items in the list, the output will be continued on the next line. Each

comma indicates a movement to the next zone. Below, the number
10 is found at the beginning of the third zone because the data in
zone one extend into zone two. The comma has thus advanced the
output to the next zone.

```
100 PRINT "This has 22 characters. ", "10"
```

This has 22 characters.   10

Successive commas cause zones to be skipped.

```
100 PRINT 5, , 10, , 15, , 20, , 25, , 30
```

```
                        5    10
                       15    20
                       25    30
```

Zones two and four contain blanks—or no data—because of the
double commas (,,) in the PRINT statement.

I.F.1.c   Automatic Line Continuation

Normally, the end of a PRINT statement causes a carriage-return
and a line-feed to be added to the current line. Output from two or
more consecutive PRINT statements—even with other statements
coming between them—can occur on the same line if a comma or
semicolon is inserted at the end of a PRINT statement.

```
100 A = 2
110 FOR X = 1 TO 4
120 A = A^A
130 PRINT A,
140 NEXT X
```

```
            4    16    256    65536
```

```
100 PRINT "DATA AND ";
110 PRINT "INFORMATION"
```

DATA AND INFORMATION

There are also several other items which need mention here.
Trailing zeros are usually omitted, a nuisance when dealing with
dollars and cents. Also, a decimal number greater than six digits
in length is normally printed as an exponent, followed by the letter

E. Both of these conventions may be circumvented by editing the output variable.

I.F.1.d TAB(X)

The TAB(X) function is used to move the cursor, or the printer head, to a certain position. It works much the same as tabulator stops on a standard typewriter by causing the next print position to be the same as the value of X.

```
100 PRINT TAB(25); "POSITION 25"

100 PRINT "COL. 1"; TAB(20); "COL. 2"; TAB(40); "COL. 3"
```

TAB's may be used several times in one PRINT statement. The argument must, however, be large enough so that the next position is to the right of the current print position.

Two minor quirks are sometimes found in BASIC systems. First, many systems start in column 0, rather than column 1. This means that TAB(25) really indicates print position 27 for a positive number. With a little experimentation and practice, such idiosyncrasies become manageable and seldom cause problems.

I.F.2 Editing Formats: PRINT USING/IMAGE

PRINT USING statements are important for formatting output data. They are not difficult to use. But since there are quite a few significant differences between versions of BASIC, it is always best to first read through the manuals. A quick glance is usually all it takes to understand where and how the PRINT USING statements are used. The following examples are highly generalized to serve as an overview. They will, however, work as is on some systems, and with minor modifications on most other systems. These paragraphs should not be taken lightly. The programmer and the analyst see the program, but the USER has to live with the output.

1. ln : format
   ln PRINT USING ln; list

   ```
   10 : $###.##
   100 PRINT USING 10; A
   ```

2. ln IMAGE$ = "format"
   ln PRINT USING IMAGE$; list

   ```
   10 IMAGE$ = "$###.##"
   100 PRINT USING IMAGE$; A
   ```

3. In PRINT USING format;

      100 PRINT USING "$###.##"; A

This set of examples gives an indication of the wide range of possibilities for the PRINT USING statement. In the first example, the editing format is entered on a separate line. Sucessive PRINT USING statements then refer to the line number where the needed format is to be found. The second example is much the same, except a variable 'IMAGE$' is used instead of the line number. The third example shows the editing format on the same line as the PRINT USING statement.

None of the three examples is particularly better than the others, but the first two do permit the same editing format to be referenced more than once, without retyping the whole format.

The PRINT USING statement must contain at least one valid editing field (format), and it is usually enclosed in quotes. The format field is also usually separated from the list by a semicolon or a comma. These act as separators only, and have little effect on the printed output. Normal spacing conventions remain in effect for the list.

A problem can result if a PRINT USING statement is to occur within an output line rather than on a line by itself. The resulting syntax error can be avoided by using multiple print lines.

```
100 PRINT "Final Payment of ";
110 PRINT USING "$#,###.##"; AMOUNT;
120 PRINT "Is Enclosed. "
```

      Final Payment of $127.82 Is Enclosed.

I.F.2.a Numerical Formats

\#   The pound sign reserves spaces   "###";12 = 12
     for a digit or a minus sign.   "###";256 = 256

.   One period can occur within a   "###.##"; 12 = 12.00
    numeric format. It indicates   "###.##"; 12.757 = 12.76
    where the decimal point is to
    be printed. If there are more
    digits to the right of the
    decimal than there are spaces
    reserved, rounding will occur
    to fit the spaces reserved.

,	The comma causes commas to be inserted before every third digit to the left of the decimal.	"#,###.##";12 = 12.00 "#,###.##";4768.65 = 4,768.65
-	A dash reserves a space for a minus sign. It is the last character in the format string, and prints a minus after negative numbers, and a space after positive numbers.	"##.##-";12 = 12.00 "##.##-"; -12.76 = 12.76-
$ $$	Dollar signs at the beginning of a decimal field reserves spaces for a dollar sign to the left of the field. Two dollar signs at the beginning of the field result in a floating dollar sign, which will appear before the left-most digit.	"$$###.##";12 = $12.00 "$$###.##";127.86 = $127.86
**	Two asterisks result in the leftmost side of the field being filled with two asterisks. They replace leading blanks.	"**###.##"; 12 = **12.00
^^^^	Four carets (up-arrows) specify E notation, or scientific notation. They must be the last characters in a field.	"#.###^^^^";.0148 = .148E-01

[Other possibilities include use of !,\ ,&, and '.]

IMPORTANT   "%"

If a number will not fit into the specified format field, digits *will be truncated* to the size of the field. The number will then be preceded by the percent sign "%", or in some cases even replaced by asterisks "***". Output should always be carefully checked.

"#,###.##";12847.62 = %2847

I.F.2.b   String Formats

'   A single quote starts a string format field, and reserves one space.

L   Each L reserves one character position. The number of Ls, plus the leading quote, determines the size of the field. The data is left justified; and if necessary, the right side will be truncated.

R   As L above, except with right justification and left truncation.

C   As L above, except the data is centered if they are smaller than the field. If necessary, data will be left justified.

100 PRINT USING "'LLL"; "ABCD", "AB", "ABCDE"

ABCD AB ___ ABCD

100 PRINT USING "'RRR"; "ABCD", "AB", "ABCDE"

ABCD ___AB BCDE

100 PRINT USING "'CCC"; "ABCD", "AB", "ABCDE"

ABCD _AB_ ABCD

[Other possibilities include use of &,\ ,!, and '.]

I.G   REVIEW QUESTIONS

1. What is a variable name? Explain the difference between numeric and string variables.
2. What are the BASIC symbols for mathematical operations? What is meant by the term *hierarchy* as it is used in this chapter?
3. Explain GOTO and GOSUB statements.

4. How are nested loops formed? What special rules must be observed?

5. How are READ and INPUT statements different? When is each best used?

6. Explain the results of each of the following:

   PRINT A; B   PRINT A, B   PRINT A; B;
   PRINT A, B;   PRINT A, B,   PRINT A, , , B

7. For the particular BASIC version you will be using, give examples for the equivalent of the PRINT USING statement.

I.H   EXERCISES

1. Write a program that averages five students' grades, and print the average on the terminal. Use your own data.

2. Using IF statements, modify the above program to print a grade for each student. (A = 90 – 100; B = 80 – 89, etc.)

NAME	SCORE	GRADE
Ron Rabine	91.75	A

3. Using FOR..NEXT statements, READ and search DATA statements to find data on a name submitted from a terminal.

   Enter Name of person => Kay Lawson

   Grades for Kay Lawson are 94 88 76 92; avg = 87.5

   DATA Kay Lawson,94,88,76,92

4. Write a payroll program that calculates the pay (gross) for an employee. The gross will include regular pay, overtime pay, plus any bonuses. Taxes are according to the following list:

AMOUNT	FEDERAL	STATE	FICA
__ 200	.20	.10	.05
__ 300	.25	.13	.07
__ 500	.275	.135	.075
501 __	"illegal amount"		

The ouput should be similar to the following format:

NAME	REG.	OVERTIME	FED.	STATE	FICA	FINAL
Morrow, D.	***.**	***.**	**.**	**.**	**.**	$***.**
Totals	******.**	*****.**	*****.**	*****.**	****.**	$*******.**

[Hint: Create the sample output first. Then prepare the necessary input data.]

II

Tables, Arrays, and Functions

Experienced programmers consider tables and arrays to be simple programming tools, easy to use and easy to understand. This is because programmers use tables and arrays for so many applications that they become skillful in their design and use. Indeed, there is hardly a chapter in this text in which tables and arrays are not used in one form or another.

The following review of tables and arrays should be read with care. It is not that tables and arrays are difficult for beginning programmers. They are not. But with the many new concepts and rules in an introductory course or text, they often seem to be regarded as something extra, or even something a little clever. This chapter offers a good opportunity for pause and review of these two important programming tools.

Also included in this chapter are sections on numeric and string functions. Numeric functions are presented here as a review, and include those numeric functions normally found in beginning texts. String functions are introduced at this point because they are, in reality, functions, and because they are important for data manipulation. A knowledge of string functions can prove extremely useful in developing data management systems, especially on the small microcomputers. Actual codes and formats may differ from vendor to vendor, but underlying structures remain the same.

II.A TABLES AND ARRAYS

Tables, or lists, are quite often defined as *one-dimensional* arrays. They are used to keep lists of related data items for quick and easy reference. Each item in a table is called an *element* of the table, and the logical location of the element within the table is indicated by a *subscripted variable*—or number.

Table 'ANIMALS$'

```
(1) |  COW   |
(2) |  GOAT  |
(3) | HORSE  |
```

In this example, the list is named ANIMALS$, and the elements within the list are the values (COW, GOAT, HORSE). Thus, 'HORSE' is the value of the third element in the list. It can be directly referenced by the form: ANIMALS$(3), where 3 is a subscript indicating the third element. ANIMALS$(1) references the value 'COW', and ANIMALS$(2) the value "GOAT".

If we know in advance that X = 3, then we can also write ANIMALS$(X) to reference the third element in the list.

```
100 LET X = 3
110 PRINT ANIMALS$ (X)
```

results in 'HORSE' being printed.

Arrays are similar to tables, except that they are *multidimensional*. They are also called matricies, but this term is usually limited to mathematical applications.

ARRAY 'TOOLS$'

COLUMNS

ROWS	(1)	(2)	(3)
(1)	BUCKET	14795	2.25
(2)	MOP	26795	4.50
(3)	SOAP	18693	3.75

The array 'TOOLS' is composed of nine elements, arranged in three rows of three columns each. Each column represents a logical relationship. Column 1 contains the names of items, column 2 the inventory number, and column 3 the price per item. Each row then contains data about a single product.

Array elements are referenced first by row number and then by column number.

ARRAY (R, C)

In the above example, TOOLS$(2,3) would reference the value "4.50". It is in row 2, the third column over. TOOLS$(2,2) references the value "26795", etc.

II.A.1   Dimension Statements: DIM

Before tables or arrays can be referenced by a program statement, enough storage space for the table or array must first be reserved. This is usually done early in the program by use of DIMension statements. A maximum size for the table or array is calculated (or estimated) and added—along with a variable name—to the dimension statement.

ln DIM (R, C)

10 DIM CARDS (5 , 5)

10 DIM CODES (4 , 4) , TOOLS$ (3 , 3)

"CODES" does not end with a dollar sign and can only contain numeric values. These values will be treated as are values of all other numeric variables. They can be used in mathematical equations. On the other hand, "TOOLS$" ends with the dollar sign, and its elements are treated as string variables.

It is also important to remember that once an array or table is defined by the dimension statement, its size remains constant. If values are not at some point assigned to the individual elements, space will nonetheless often be reserved by the system. Overstating the need for storage space is potentially wasteful.

At the same time, once the space reserved for an array or a table is full, no further data can be added. It is possible to replace or change values, but full is full. Any attempt to add more data will result in a *subscript out of range* error. Then either the dimension statement must be changed or the flowchart of the program examined to determine if a loop is repeating itself too many times or if the subscript is not being reset to some beginning point.

On some systems there also exist a row(0) and a column(0). In these systems, CARDS(4,4) would define an array with 25 elements, instead of 16. Many programmers elect to ignore the 0 rows and columns because they prefer a one-to-one logical relation between their data items and their storage spaces. On larger machines, this approach makes little difference, but on some micros, when internal storage is at a premium, it is a good idea to examine how and where elements are being stored.

A table, or list, has no column numbers, because there is only one column available. The dimension statement contains only row size.

```
10 DIMENSION NAMES$(50),GRADES(50)
```

Note the difference caused by the dollar signs. Also remember that, on some systems, 51 storage positions for 51 elements would be created.

II.A.2 Building Tables and Arrays: FOR/NEXT

Once space has been reserved for an array or a table, data can then be stored in the reserved space. The DIMension statement alone does not put data in the reserved area. It is up to the program to assign data to the space reserved by the DIMension statement. And once the program assigns data to a storage position, the data remains there until it is overwritten or the program is terminated.

For the table in Section II.A, ANIMALS$, there are three data items to be stored: COW, GOAT, and HORSE. Space for the tables is first allocated by a DIMension statement, and the data items are then read into the tables.

```
10  DIM ANIMALS$ (3)
```

```
100 FOR X = 1 TO 3
110        READ ANIMALS$ (X)
120 NEXT X
```

```
1000 DATA COW, GOAT, HORSE
```

The value of X is first set to 1, and the first data item 'COW' is read into ANIMALS$(X). Since X = 1, this is equivalent to reading 'COW' into ANIMALS$(1). X is next set to 2, and the process continues until X reaches the limit of 3.

To print the values of the data items once they are in the table, simply use PRINT instead of READ. Also add any line editing features needed, such as ',' or ';'.

```
100 FOR X = 1 TO 3
110        PRINT ANIMALS$ (X) ,
120 NEXT X
```

The comma at the end of line 110 causes the values to be printed in columns.

```
    COW        GOAT         HORSE
```

For the array, TOOLS$, the same procedure is followed, except that there are now two levels of subscripts instead of one. Nested loops are used in this case, one loop for each level.

```
10 DIM TOOLS$ (3,3)
```

```
100 FOR X = 1 TO 3
110     FOR Y = 1 TO 3
120         READ TOOLS$ (X, Y)
130     NEXT Y
140 NEXT X
```

```
1000 DATA BUCKET, 14795, 2.25, MOP, 26795, 5.40
1010 DATA SOAP, 18693, 3.75
```

Here, X is first set to 1 (row 1). Then Y is set to 1 (column 1) and the value 'BUCKET' is read. Then Y is set to 2, and '14795' read, etc., until the value of Y reaches the limit of 3. Then X is set to 2, Y is reset to 1, and the process is repeated.

The values stored in the array can then be printed by changing READ to PRINT and adding any desired editing features.

II.A.3   Searching Tables and Arrays: FOR/NEXT

If we know the inventory number of a product is '18693', then by matching the value of an element against this constant, it is possible to reference related data.

```
100 FOR X = 1 to 3
110 IF TOOLS$ (X, 2)  =  '18693' THEN 200
120 NEXT X
130 PRINT "ERROR. . . . "
  .
  .
  .
200 PRINT TOOLS$ (X, 1) ,  "PRICE = "; TOOLS$ (X, 3)
```

The value of X will first be set to 1, and TOOLS$(1,2) checked to determine if it equals 18693. Since it does not (it equals 14975), X is incremented by one and TOOLS$(2,2) checked, etc. TOOLS$(3,3) does equal 18693, and the program skips to line 200, with X being equal to 3. Thus, TOOLS$(X,1) will reference the value 'SOAP', and TOOLS$(X,3) the value '3.75'.

For clarity, the above example might also be written as follows:

```
50 LET NAME = 1 \ LET NUMBER = 2 \ LET PRICE = 3

100 FOR X = 1 TO 3
110     IF TOOLS$ (X, NUMBER)  =  "18693" THEN 200
120 NEXT X
130 PRINT "ERROR. . . . "

200 PRINT TOOLS$ (X, NAME) ,  "PRICE = "; TOOLS$ (X, PRICE)
```

II.A.4   Updating Array Values

When we want to change the value of an element in an array, the new value is assigned to the location of the element in the array. In this way, the old value is replaced with the new value.

```
400 LET TOOLS$ (X, PRICE)  =  '4. 25'
```

If it were desirable to use PRICE in a mathematical formula, it would first be necessary to convert "4.25" to a numerical value (v. the VAL() function). In some instances it might prove useful to DIMension two arrays: one for alphameric values and one for numeric values. Data values in the two arrays can be correlated.

400 PRINT TOOLS$(X, NAME), TOOLS(X, PRICE)

II.B MATRIX FUNCTIONS: MAT

Almost every Standard BASIC text contains a chapter on MATRIX statements. They are, therefore, presented here in a fairly complete list, with the most common at the top of the list.

In very general terms, a one- or two-dimensional array is also called a matrix in computer texts. This is simply because it contains subscripted variables, and no further mathematical claims are ever made. Matrix functions simply provide a quick method for inputting and outputting data (to be) stored in arrays. They can also be used in some mathematical operations. The real value of matrix statements is that, once an array has been defined by the dimension statement, entire matrices can be manipulated with single statements.

ln MAT verb

ln MAT array-name = operation

(1) ln MAT INPUT array-name

Inputs data from a terminal, row by row, into a previously defined matrix.

100 MAT INPUT N

100 MAT INPUT N (R, C)

(2) ln MAT READ array-name

Reads data from DATA statements, row by row, into a previously defined matrix.

100 MAT READ N

100 MAT READ N (R, C)

```
10 DIM TOOLS$ (3, 3)

100 MAT READ TOOLS$

1000 DATA BUCKET, 14795, 2. 25, MOP, 26795, 5. 40
1010 DATA SOAP, 18693, 3. 75
```

(3) ln MAT PRINT array-name;
     ln MAT PRINT array-name,
     ln MAT PRINT array-name

> Prints the contents of a matrix
> on the terminal or on the line
> printer. The semicolon separates
> each element with a space, and
> starts each row on a new line.
> A comma prints each element in a
> new zone, each row on a new line;
> and the third statement (no
> semicolon or comma) puts each
> element on a new line.

```
100 MAT PRINT N;

100 MAT PRINT N,

100 MAT PRINT N

   100 MAT PRINT TOOLS$

100 MAT PRINT N (R, C)

100 MAT PRINT N (R, C)

100 MAT PRINT N (R, C)
```

(4) ln MAT array-name-2 = array-name-1

> Causes the contents of array-name-2
> to be equal to those of array-name-1.
> The contents of array-name-1 are not
> altered.

```
100 MAT N2 = N1

100 MAT N2 (R, C) = N1 (R, C)
```

$$(5) \ \text{ln MAT array-name} = \begin{matrix} \text{CON} \\ \text{ZER} \\ \text{IDN} \end{matrix}$$

> CON causes ones to be put into all elements of the array.
>
> ZER causes zeros to be put into all elements of the array.
>
> IDN sets up an identity matrix with diagonals equal to ones, and nondiagonals equal to zeros.

100 MAT N = CON

100 MAT N = ZER

100 MAT N = IDN

$$(6) \ \text{ln MAT array-name-3} = \text{array-name-1} \begin{bmatrix} + \\ - \\ * \end{bmatrix} \text{array-name-2}$$

> Adds, subtracts, or multiplies array-name-1 to or from, or by array-name-2 and puts the results in array-name-3.

100 MAT N3 = N1 + N2

100 MAT N3 = N1 - N2

100 MAT N3 = N1 * N2

$$(7) \ \text{ln MAT array-name-2} = \begin{matrix} \text{INV (array-name-1)} \\ \text{TRN (array-name-1)} \end{matrix}$$

> Inverts, or transposes, array-name-1 and puts the results in array-name-2.

100 MAT N2 = INV (N1)

100 MAT N2 = TRN (N1)

(8) ln MAT array-name-2 = (X) * array-name-1

> Multiplies the elements in array-name-1 by the value X (scalar multiplication)

and puts the results in array-name-2.
X must be a mathematical expression
and must be enclosed in parentheses.

100 MAT N2 = (N3/2) * N1

II.C   NUMERIC FUNCTIONS

In much the same manner as MATRIX functions provide quick
and easy access to several otherwise involved mathematical operations, NUMERIC FUNCTIONS supply several mathematical and
trigonometric functions which are easier to use than to create.
BASIC also provides a means whereby programmers can define
their own numeric functions. The former are called BUILT-IN,
INTERNAL, or LIBRARY FUNCTIONS. The latter are referred
to as USER-DEFINED FUNCTIONS.

String functions, which may also be user defined, are discussed
in the next section of this chapter.

II.C.1   RND, SQR, SGN, SIN, COS, TAN, ATN, LOG, INT

(1)   RND(X)   Usually returns a decimal
                                  value between 0.0 and 1.0.
           RANDOM   On some systems, X is the
                                  upper limit, with values
       100 N = RND(10)   falling between 1 and X.
                                  Some systems require the
                                  verb RANDOM to occur be-
                                  fore a statement with
                                  RND if different
                                  random numbers are
                                  to be generated within a
                                  single run.

   100 X = INT ((RND*100)+.5)   When Rnd returns decimal
                                  values (for example, .0001
                                  to .9999), then the function
                                  must be modified.

(2)   SQR(X)   Returns square root of X.

       100 N = SQR(X)

(3)   SGN(X)   Returns -1 if X is negative,
                                             0 if X is equal to zero, and
          100 S = SGN(X)   1 if X is positive.

(4)   SIN(X)   Finds the sine, cosine, tan-
             COS(X)   gent, or arctangent of X. X is
             TAN(X)   given in radians.
             ATN(X)

          100 S = SIN(X)

(5)   LOG(X)   Returns the natural log of X.

          100 L = LOG(X)

(6)   INT(X)   Truncation. Returns greatest
                                             integer of X—i.e., without
          100 I = INT(X)   places to the right of the decimal.

      100 I = INT(X + 0.5)   X is rounded to the nearest whole
                                             number.

II.D   STRINGS

Strings are comprised of a connected sequence of characters, or
bytes, and are considered to be a single data item.

II.D.1   Dynamic Strings

If a string is assigned a value, the size of the

```
100 LET TITLE$ = "ADVANCED BASIC"
200 LET TITLE$ = "RUNNING"
```

string is determined by the number of characters in the string. The
string "TITLE$" in line 100 contains 14 characters, while the string
in line 200 contains 7 characters. In this example, the string is said
to be dynamic. Its length may or may not change, depending upon
the value assigned to it.

II.D.2   Fixed-Length Strings

In MAP statements, as well as in virtual arrays, the length of a
string is fixed. MAPs are discussed in the next chapter, and it is

sufficient to note here the manner in which the variables in line 100 are assigned a predetermined size. While the length of the data within the variable may change, the variable's length will remain the same. The string variable is said to be a fixed-length variable. If the value assigned a fixed-length string variable is smaller than the variable, the rest of the field will be padded with blanks.

NOTE:

```
100 MAP (DATA_REC)   LAST_NAME$   = 20% &
                    , FIRST_NAME$ = 15% &
                    , INITIAL     =  2% &
150                                           REM
200 MAP (DATA_REC) FULL_NAME$     = 37%
250                                           REM
300 INPUT "LAST NAME = => "; LAST_NAME$
310 INPUT "FIRST NAME = => "; FIRST_NAME$
320 INPUT "INITIAL (I.) = => "; INITIAL$
400 PRINT
510 PRINT FULL_NAME$
```

with the result:

```
LAST NAME = => JONES
FIRST NAME = => RITA
INITIAL (I.) = => S.

JONES            RITA            S.
```

The INPUT statements in lines 300, 310, and 320 accept data from the terminal, but because the lengths of the fields are fixed in line 100, each value entered is left-justified within the field, and, where necessary, the rest of the field is padded with blanks. This results in the spacing in the output line.

II.D.3 Justifying Data LSET/RSET

Once a string variable has been defined or otherwise created, data can be assigned to the variable, while the length of the variable remains unchanged.

A LET statement causes a string variable to become the length of the characters assigned to it.

```
100 LET LETTERS$ = "ABC"
```

```
200 LET LETTERS$ = "ABCDE"
```

In the first example, LETTERS$ will contain three characters (ABC) and be three characters in length. In the second example, LETTERS$ will contain five characters (ABCDE) and be five characters in length.

The size of the variable remains unchanged, however, when LSET and RSET are used to assign data to a string. LSET left-justifies the data within the string:

```
100 LET LETTERS$ = "ABCDE"
110 LSET LETTERS$ = "123"
120 PRINT LETTERS$ + "END"
```

with the result:

```
123 END
```

RSET works in the same manner, except that the data is right-justified:

```
100 LET LETTERS$ = "ABCDE"
110 RSET LETTERS$ = "123"
120 PRINT "START" + LETTERS$
```

with the result:

```
START 123
```

In both examples, the data string "123" is justified within the string and the remaining spaces padded with blanks. The variable LETTERS$ thus retains its original size of five characters.

String variables defined in MAP statements are no different. LSET and RSET move data to the storage area defined by the MAP statement and pad any remaining spaces with blanks.

Should the data string, however, be longer than the assigned string variable, the data will be truncated to fit the length of the variable. This means that characters are deleted from the string.

```
100 LET LETTERS$ = "ABCDE"
110 RSET LETTERS$ = "TUVWXYZ"
120 PRINT LETTERS$
```

with the result:

```
VWXYZ
```

and conversely:

```
100 LET LETTERS$ = "ABCDE"
110 LSET LETTERS$ = "TUVWXYZ"
120 PRINT LETTERS$
```

with the result:

TUVWX

LSET and RSET are often used in entering new data for storage in MAP-defined areas. For example, a program to build a file of names and addresses might look like this:

```
100 MAP (NEWREC)     NAME$    = 25% &
                   , ADDRESS$ = 25% &
                   , CITY$    = 15% &
                   , STATE$   =  2% &
                   , ZIP      =  5
150                                              REM
200 OPEN . . .
250                                              REM
300 LINPUT "ENTER NAME       = =>"; IN_NAME$
310 LINPUT "ENTER ADDRESS    = =>"; IN_ADDRESS$
320 LINPUT "ENTER CITY       = =>"; IN_CITY$
330 INPUT  "STATE            = =>"; IN_STATE$
340 INPUT  "ZIP              = =>"; ZIP
350                                              REM
400 LSET NAME$ = IN_NAME$
410 LSET ADDRESS$ = IN_ADDRESS$
420 LSET CITY$ = IN_CITY$
430 LSET STATE$ = IN_STATE$
450                                              REM
500 PUT . . .     \ GOTO 300
```

This program is minimal and much remains to be added, but it indicates how data can be justified within a predefined string. The string will always begin in the same column and either it will contain enough blanks to pad the field, or the data will have been truncated to fit the field.

II.E   STRING FUNCTIONS

Like the numeric functions reviewed in Chapter II, built-in string functions supply preprogrammed operations, which are easier to use than to create. String manipulation functions are an important part of BASIC and help to form simple commands that are easy to understand and use. The following paragraphs are limited in possble examples, but only because the actual uses for these statements in data and information systems are almost endless.

Note that when numeric values are returned by the function, the function name is *not* followed by a dollar sign. When a string is returned, however, the function name ends with a dollar sign.

II.E.1   Determining Length   LEN

LEN returns the number of characters within a string.

```
ln  verb LEN(string)
```

```
100 LET LETTERS$ = "ABCDE"
110 PRINT LEN(LETTERS$)
```

with the result:

```
5
```

This function also works for data stored in virtual arrays because trailing blanks are automatically stripped when a string is retrieved from the array. LEN always returns a numeric value, and in many instances it is useful to save this value for later reference:

```
100 LINPUT "ENTER LETTERS      "; LETTERS$
110 NUMB = LEN(LETTERS$)
120 FOR X = 1 TO NUMB . . . .
```

NUMB will contain the number of characters entered from the terminal. Additional statements can then be written to examine or process each character in turn until the string is completely processed.

II.E.2   Determining Position   POS

In processing data, it is often useful to know the location of a character or substring within a string. Once located, they can then be extracted for further processing.

```
ln verb POS(string, substring, begin)
```

STRING is the string to be searched, SUBSTRING is the data to be searched for, and BEGIN is the position within the string at which the search is to begin. If the substring is found, the position of its first character will be returned. If the substring is not found, the value 0 will be returned.

```
100 LET LETTERS$ = "ABCDE"
110 LET SUB$ = "BCD"
120 LET BCD% = POS (LETTERS$, SUB$, 1%)
130 PRINT BCD%
```

with the result:

2

or

```
100 LET SUB$ = "XYZ"
120 LET BCD% = POS (LETTERS$, SUB$, 1%)
```

with the result:

0

(These examples will also work without the percent sign: %.)

II.E.3   Converting to Numeric Values   VAL

VAL(string) causes string data to be converted to numeric values. This is often necessary when data has been entered in string format, but needs to be used mathematically.

```
ln  verb variable = VAL (string)
```

```
400 PRINT VAL (TOOLS$ (1, 3) )  + VAL (TOOLS$ (2, 3) )  + VAL (TOOLS$ (3, 3) )
```

II.E.4   Extracting Substrings   LEFT$/RIGHT$

LEFT$ and RIGHT$ extract substrings from the left or from the right of data strings.

```
ln verb LEFT$ (string, number)
```

```
ln verb RIGHT$ (string, position)
```

When used with LEFT$, NUMBER indicates the number of characters to be extracted, beginning with the first character.

```
100 LET LETTERS$ = "ABCDE"
110 PRINT LEFT$ (LETTERS$, 2%)
```

with the result:

AB

When using RIGHT$, however, the starting POSITION within the string is given. All characters beginning with this position to the end of the string will be returned.

```
100 LET LETTERS$ = "ABCDE"
110 PRINT RIGHT$ (LETTERS$, 2%)
```

with the result:

BCDE

The slight difference between these functions should be noted. LEFT$ returns a number of characters beginning with the leftmost character, while RIGHT$ returns all characters beginning at a given position.

II.E.5   Extracting Substrings   MID$/SEG$

MID$ extracts a substring by beginning at a certain position within the string and extracting a number of characters.

ln verb MID$ (string, begin, number)

STRING is the string from which the substring is to be extracted, BEGIN indicates the starting position, and NUMBER is the number of characters to be extracted.

```
100 LET LETTERS$ = "ABCDE"
110 PRINT SEG$ (LETTERS$, 2%, 3%)
```

with the result:

BCD

SEG$ can also be used to extract substrings. Its use seems at first glance, to be complex, but it is recommended as an alternative to the preceding three functions.   It is sometimes easier to understand and use a single command, especially when the other statements pose differing requirements.

ln verb SEG$(string, begin, end)

STRING is the string from which the characters are to be extracted, BEGIN is the starting position, and END is the last position in the string.
    Note the following examples:

```
100 LET LETTERS$ = "ABCDE"
110 PRINT SEG$ (LETTERS$, 2%, 4%)
```

with the result:

BCD

and

```
110 PRINT SEG$ (LETTERS$, 1%, 3%)
```

with the result:

ABC

and

```
110 PRINT SEG$ (LETTERS$, 3%, LEN (LETTERS$) )
```

with the result:

CDE

In these examples, SEG$ produces the same results as MID$, LEFT$, and RIGHT$, respectively. In all three cases, the string itself is left intact and can be further referenced within the program.

II.E.6   Creating Identical Strings   SPACE$/STRING$

Both SPACE$ and STRING$ create strings of identical characters. The only difference between the two is that while SPACE$ can be expected to create a string of blanks, STRING$ will have to be told which character is to be used.

ln verb = SPACE$(length)

ln verb = STRING$(length, ASCII-value)

100 LET LETTERS$ = "ABCDE"
110 PRINT SEG$(LETTERS$, 1%, 2%) + SPACE$(3) + "END"

with the result:

AB   END
(2 spaces between AB and END)

100 PRINT STRING$(5%, 42%)

with the result:

*****

(a five-character string is created using the ASCII character equal to the ASCII value 42; i.e., the special character
*)

II.E.7   Removing Trailing Blanks   TRM$

TRM$ removes trailing blanks from a string. It is primarily used
to retrieve strings which have been padded with blanks and stored
in an array and mapped field.

ln verb TRM$(string)

100 LET LETTERS$ = "ABCDE   "
110 PRINT TRM$(LETTERS$) + "END"

with the result:

ABCDEEND

The blanks after the E in the original string are deleted when the
string is printed, and the string END is then added to it.

II.E.8   User-Created Functions

Non-standard functions can be defined by the programmer, and
these functions can then be performed throughout the rest of the
program.   Such functions are called USER-DEFINED FUNC-

TIONS. They may be single BASIC statements or several lines in length.

```
ln  DEF FNname(argument) = formula

ln  DEF FNname(argument)
    .
    .
ln  FNEND

100 DEF FN_RADIUS(RADIUS) = 3.1415 * RADIUS^2
    .
    .
200 INPUT RADIUS
    .
    .
300 PRINT FN_RADIUS(RADIUS)

100 DEF FN_RADIUS(RADIUS)
110 FN_RADIUS = 3.1415 * RADIUS^2
120 FNEND
    .
    .
200 INPUT RADIUS
    .
    .
300 PRINT FN_RADIUS(RADIUS)
```

Note the function name, FN_RADIUS, has 'FN' as its first two letters. This is a must. The following characters are optional, but a function name must begin with 'FN'. Any number of arguments are permitted. The formula is also omitted from the DEF statement in multilined functions. User-defined functions are also usually listed early in the program; and it is helpful to group all DEF statements together as an aid to program maintenance.

Though often quite useful, user-defined functions are sometimes better written as small subroutines. Subroutines are, in the end, more versatile and often easier to decipher.

II.F REVIEW QUESTIONS

    1. Why are tables and arrays used in computer programs? How do they help the programmer?

2. Where must the DIMENSION statement be put in a BASIC program? Why?

3. What would be indicated by the error message "Subscript out of range"? What would you look for to correct this error?

4. What would be the difference between the array names 'BOOK' and 'BOOKS'?

5. How do you know on your system how many storage positions are in a table or an array?

6. What are functions? Explain the similarities and differences among MATRIX, STRING, and NUMERIC functions.

7. What are library functions? User-defined functions?

8. Carefully examine the explanation for dynamic and fixed-length strings. How might MAP statements be used to control printer spacing?

9. What is meant by the phrase "justifying data"?

10. Examine the various string functions and note that some end with a dollar sign. How might you predict when a function will contain with this sign?

II.G EXERCISES

1. Store the data for a small class of students in an array, six by three (6,3). Leave the final column blank. Then print a class list.

NAME	CLASS	FINAL AVG
Dow, Gary	SR	
Fanich, Kay	SOPH	
Hall, James	JR	
Manning, Claus	SOPH	
Petty, Sharon	SR	
Soral, Linda	JR	

2. Create a second array to hold the course averages for each student.

88,87,93,81,77
93,91,88,87,82
86,77,72,81,73
91,88,62,91,80
77,73,81,72,65
91,87,86,76,82

Compute the final average, rounded, for each student, and then store the result in the array created in 1 above. Print out the class list with the final averages.

3. Print a list of all seniors from the class list. Using the data already stored in the first array, create the following format. Grades: A = 90-100, B = 80-89, etc.

LAST NAME	FIRST INITIAL	FINAL GRADE
Dow	G.	A

4. Write a program that permits the instructor to change any of the students' grades from the terminal. Be as efficient as possible.

5. Load 52 playing cards into an array. Using the random number function, deal two hands of cards. Be sure no duplicates are dealt!

III

Data, Characters, and Maps

III.A DATA TYPES

One of the earliest lessons one must learn in order to write a program in BASIC is to distinguish data types. For the beginning student with limited programming experience, this usually means a distinction between NUMERIC and STRING classifications. In this chapter, additional distinctions among data types are presented and their use in MAP statements discussed. This chapter also contains an introduction to data strings and built-in string functions.

III.A.1 Numeric/Alphameric Variables

Numeric variables may only contain the numbers 0 though 9; and string variables may contain all of the characters on the keyboard, including the numbers. A common rule states that a variable containing string data must end with the dollar sign: '$', and that a variable containing numeric data *cannot* end with a '$'. Only the latter, however, can be used in mathematical operations.

```
A1 = Numeric Variable

A2$ = String (or alphameric) Variable
```

This distinction has, of course, to do with how the data is to be stored and processed. Also, string variables are often said to be manipulated while numeric variables are reserved for the usual arithmetic operations—addition, multiplication, subtraction, and division.

NOTE:

```
100 LET A1 = 2
200 LET A2$ = "2"
300 LET A1 = A1 + A1
400 LET A2$ = A2$ + A2$
500 PRINT "A1 = "; A1
600 PRINT "A2$ = "; A2$
```

with the result:

```
A1 = 4
A2$ = 22
```

The operations in lines 300 and 400 produce quite different results. The variables are defined as containing different *data types* .

When constructing algorithms to manipulate or mathematically process data, it is useful to carefully consider how each data element will be used and to make a correspondingly correct assignment of a variable name. Let it be sufficient to state that these two data types are stored differently by the computer, and processes affecting them are usually kept distinctly separate.

III.A.2   Numeric Constants and Variables

III.A.2.a   Integers and Integer Variables

A further distinction can be made between integer and real numeric data. Each can occur as either a variable or a constant.

An integer is a whole number and cannot contain a decimal

point; i.e., it has no fractional parts. An integer may be positive, zero, or negative.

$$25, 0, -25 = \text{integers}$$

$$A1\% = \text{integer variable}$$

Note the use of the percent sign "%" to signify the integer variable. This convention is common in BASIC manuals, and is used in programs to enable more efficient utilization of machine and system resources.

III.A.2.b Integer Constants

An integer constant contains a string of whole numbers that have no decimal point.

$$14789, -25643 = \text{integer constants}$$

These numbers are coded directly into a program and remain the same, or constant, until changed by rewriting the code.

III.A.2.c Real Numbers and Real Variables

Real numbers, sometimes referred to as floating point numbers, are numbers that must not, but may contain a decimal point. Real numbers may also be negative or positive.

$$25.5, -25.5 = \text{real number}$$

$$\text{TOTAL} = \text{real variable}$$

No special sign may be used for real variables.

III.A.2.d Real Constants

Real constants, or floating point constants, represent a string of numbers that must have either a decimal point or a decimal exponent. They may have both.

$$14.789, -25.643 = \text{real constants}$$

Like most constants, real constants are written directly into the program and are changed by rewriting the program.

III.A.2.e Exponents

An exponent is a large number with leading or trailing zeroes that has been shortened in writing by the use of a mathematical shorthand. It is a convenient method of displaying or storing large numbers in a smaller space. The abbreviation used is the capital E. If the number containing the exponent is positive, the decimal point is moved to the right:

$$4.8E + 05 = 48,000$$

and if the exponent is negative, the decimal point is moved to the left:

$$7E - 5 = .00007$$

The only actual limits on the use of this notation are usually imposed by each individual system, and manuals should be referenced if exponentials are expected to be unusually large.

III.A.3   String Variables

A string variable contains a related sequence of characters that make up a single data item. This sequence is linear because the characters follow one another, as opposed to being in a matrix or an array. String variables must be enclosed in quotes because the blank character may be found within the string. Since all strings begin and end somewhere, and even though blanks can delimit numbers, blanks cannot be used as delimiters for strings if they can occur within the string itself. The computer would not know where related items begin and end. Quotes are therefore used to signal the beginning and end of strings.

String variables may contain letters of the alphabet, numbers, special characters, and the blank space.

"A1. Balance Due" = String Variable

III.B   VALUES

Data items are said to contain values. A value is a particular character or group of characters that is classified according to one of the data types listed above.

200 and 2.5 = values of type real numbers

"Home Sweet Home" = value of type string variable

The distinctions made in this chapter may be further refined. For the present, they form a working basis for defining and delimiting data items when processing files. Carefully considered use of variable names leads to better and more efficient programming practices.

III.C   DECLARE STATEMENTS

DECLARE statements appear only in the most recent versions of BASIC. They are included here and in the sample programs to introduce them to those not familiar with their use as a programming tool. When found in the sample programs, they can be ignored without loss to the program.

DATA TYPES can also be explicitly assigned by using the DECLARE statement. This statement permits a programmer to declare the class of value that can be attributed to a given variable name.

An assignment, or declaration, can be made only once in a program, and a variable once assigned cannot at the same time occur in the MAP or COMMON statements.

NOTE:

```
100 DECLARE STRING TITLE
200 LET TITLE = "ADVANCED BASIC"
300 PRINT TITLE
```

with the result:

```
ADVANCED BASIC
```

or:

```
100 DECLARE REAL CONSTANT PI = 3.14159
200 DECLARE REAL RADIUS
300 INPUT "ENTER RADIUS = =>"; RADIUS
400 PRINT "DIMENSION = "; PI * SQR(RADIUS)
```

with the result:

```
ENTER RADIUS = => 2.5
DIMENSION = 19.634937
```

DECLARE statements make programs easier to read as well as easier to understand. It can sometimes be disconcerting to work on a program full of "%" and "$" signs. This is especially true if one is not altogether familiar with the program. After a while, lines of code seen to swim in pools of "%" and "$" signs.

If a constant occurs often in a program and the possibility exists that its value might at some future date be changed, a single declaration for the variable at the beginning of the program assures that any changes will be easily made. Simply change the assignment in the DECLARE statement, and all subsequent occurrences of the constant will be assigned the new value.

It should be noted that while more than one integer or real variable can be declared in a single statement:

```
100 DECLARE INTEGER          &
                    SIZE     &
               , LENGTH  &
               , WIDTH
```

only one constant can be declared in a statement:

```
100 DECLARE REAL CONSTANT PI = 3.14159
200 DECLARE REAL CONSTANT RADIUS = 2.5
300 DECLARE REAL DIMENSION
400 LET DIMENSION = PI * SQR(RADIUS)
```

When designing and coding a program, it should always be remembered that at some point in time, someone may well be asked to make changes to this program—i.e., "to do maintenance". Any help the initial programmer can give by leaving a well-designed program will not only be appreciated, but also it will be an advantage both psychologically and financially.

III.D   RECORD LAYOUTS

Before programs can be written, the data to be used must be analyzed and organized. Unless one has an immediate and accurate overview of the operations to be programmed, it is never a good idea to simply start coding and then see what happens. Such an approach wastes effort and resources. An old, but still useful approach is to begin with the output and then work backward to the input.

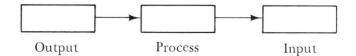

Output   Process   Input

At first glance, the above diagram may appear backward. But assume we are to produce something. Not just anything— but something. Then we must first know what it is we are to produce. And what it is must be what is wanted!

For example, if we are told we are to produce a final grade listing, we must know what will be on the listing. We need to know what the output will look like.

NAME   AVG   GRADE

Linker, Bob   88   B

Once we have a starting point, an example from which to work, we will encounter other questions. For the above grade list, we need to know how to figure the average, from where we will get the data, how much data will there be, and how to assign which grade to which average.

Process:

AVG = (GRADE1 + GRADE2 + GRADE3 + GRADE4)/ 4

GRADES: A = 90 − 100
        B = 89 − 90 etc.

Input:

DATA Linker,Bob,88,83,93,88

This example is, of course, obvious. But note that we now know that the average comes from four equally weighted grades and that a standard system is used to assign letter grades. Only at this point can the DATA be collected and organized.

The above operation would, in fact, prove quite simple, and one could program it without too many questions or a great deal of effort. And this is true for most assignments in beginning texts. In reality, programming assignments outside of the classroom are rarely this simple. They are far more complex, and each of the above steps needs careful study and thought before even the first line of code is written.

For most systems, this means documenting each step as it is completed. After the output is agreed upon, it is entered on a printer spacing chart. The various processes are then written down and will (hopefully) later be well documented within the program, and sometimes in pseudocode or in a flowchart.

The format of the input must also be documented. This is usually done in a *Record Layout Form*. These forms come in many formats, and some are quite complex. The record layouts used in this text are considered fairly standard and can be used to handle most data formats.

VARIABLE NAME	DATA TYPE	DATA SIZE	CONTENTS
FULL_NAME	A	20	Contains both first and last names
GRADE1	N	3	1st Midterm
GRADE2	N	3	2nd Midterm
GRADE3	N	3	3rd Midterm
GRADE4	N	3	Final Exam

The variable names should be exactly as they will be in the program. Data types are A for alphameric and N for numeric. Data size contains the largest number of characters permitted for the variable. This might also be coded 999, etc. Be careful here. The data size is the number of characters—not necessarily the number of storage bytes. More will be said about this in following chapters. And finally, contents are comments that might help explain the values to be assigned to each variable: for example, "Acceptable CODEs = M (male), F (female)".

Note that the variable FULL_NAME will now always be 20 characters in length. Thus FULL_NAME will equal

```
"Linker, Bob          "     [with nine blanks]
```

Note also that the various GRADEs are three characters in length, rather than two, because someone might score 100.

III.E   MAP STATEMENTS

The MAP statement allocates core memory storage. The amount of storage needed is allocated when a program is compiled and never changes. Thus, the address and size of variables remain the same at all times. Their storage space is static and predictable. Without a core dump, we do not know the addresses for our variables, but we always know their sizes in bytes.

The most common use of MAP statements is to associate fields of records stored in the I/O buffers with program variables. A MAP for a record is first laid out in a MAP statement.

III.E.1 Single MAP

Assuming a record layout for the records to be created for a sequential file named "STUDENT.DAT"

VARIABLE NAME	DATA TYPE	DATA SIZE	
LAST_NAME	A	20	JONES
FIRST_NAME	A	15	RITA
INITIAL	A	2	S.
ADDRESS	AN	20	130 PINE ST.
CITY	A	15	PITTSBURGH
STATE	A	2	PA
	A	1	BLANK
ZIP	N	5	15261

The MAP statement would read:

```
100 MAP (RECOUT)   LAST__NAME$  =  20%  &
                 , FIRST__NAME$ =  15%  &
                 , INITIAL$     =   2%  &
                 , ADDRESS$     =  20%  &
                 , CITY$        =  15%  &
                 , STATE$       =   2%  &
                 , FILL$        =   1%  &
                 , ZIP$         =   5%
```

and the buffer would look like this:

			1 BYTE	
	2 BYTES		2 BYTES	
20 BYTES	15 BYTES	20 BYTES	15 BYTES	5 BYTES
JONES	RITA	S.| 130 PINE ST.	PITTSBURGH PA	15261
LAST_NAME	FIRST_NAME	ADDRESS	CITY STATE	ZIP
	INITIAL		FILL	

Any reference to one of these variables will result in the corresponding bytes, or data, being accessed. FIRST_NAME would reference bytes 21 through 35, and STATE would reference bytes 72 through 73.

```
100 PRINT FIRST_NAME$; STATE$
```

would result in

```
RITA            PA
```

NOTE: Eleven spaces are between 'RITA' and 'PA' because FIRST_NAME has been defined in the MAP statement above as containing 15 bytes. The field has 15 characters even though 'RITA' only has 4 characters. The rest are blanks.

The name associated with the MAP defined above in the parentheses is 'RECOUT', with each field being given a variable name and a size allocation. Any further reference to this MAP can be done using the name 'RECOUT'.

For a program that would input data from a terminal and create the file named above "STUDENT.DAT", one would use the following steps:

1. Layout the record with a MAP.
2. OPEN and define the file.
3. Input the data.
4. Format and write the records.
5. Close the file.

We will need to be sure and associate the MAP for the records in step 1 with the file opened in step 2. This is done as an option to the OPEN statement with

```
MAP RECOUT
```

Variables defined in the MAP statement are now associated with the file 'STUDENT.DAT'.

Our program would look like this:

```
100 MAP (RECOUT)    LAST__NAME$   =   20% &
                  , FIRST__NAME$  =   15% &
                  , INITIAL$      =    2% &
                  , ADDRESS$      =   20% &
                  , CITY$         =   15% &
                  , STATE$        =    2% &
                  , FILL$         =    1% &
                  , ZIP$          =    5%
150                                                            REM
200 OPEN 'STUDENT.DAT'                        &
         FOR OUTPUT AS FILE #1                &
       , MAP RECOUT
210                                                            REM
300 INPUT "FIRST__NAME (STOP) ==>        "; FIRST__NAME$
310 IF FIRST__NAME$ = "STOP" THEN 600
320 INPUT "INITIAL (I.)        ==> "; INITIAL$
330 INPUT "LAST NAME           ==> "; LAST__NAME$
340 INPUT "STREET ADDRESS      ==> "; ADDRESS$
350 INPUT "CITY                ==> "; CITY$
360 INPUT "STATE (AA)          ==> "; STATE$
370 INPUT "ZIP                 ==> "; ZIP$
400 PUT #1
500 GOTO 300
550                                                            REM
600 LET LAST__NAME$ = "END-OF-FILE"
610 PUT #1
700 CLOSE #1
800 END
```

In this program, the data is entered in a different order than it will be stored within the record. Note that one PUT statement automatically moves all of the data as defined in the MAP. There is no need for LET statements or other levels of intermediate assignment.

On the other hand, BASIC does not create, or initialize, variables that have been defined, or named, in MAP statements. This means that MAP statements must occur in the program before any references are made to them or their contents. Note also that FILL$ is used to define unused space in the record.

III.E.2 Multiple MAPs

It is often desirable to access data stored in a buffer in more than one way. This is perhaps the easiest way to extract data from a string or to join—i.e., concatenate—two strings. The second MAP is said to "overlay" the first.

```
100 MAP (RECOUT)     LAST_NAME$   =   20%  &
                    ,FIRST_NAME$  =   15%  &
                    ,INITIAL$     =    2%  &
                    ,ADDRESS$     =   20%  &
                    ,CITY$        =   15%  &
                    ,STATE$       =    2%  &
                    ,FILL$        =    1%  &
                    ,ZIP$         =    5%
150                                                                 REM
200 MAP (RECOUT) FULL_NAME$     = 37% &
                ,FULL_ADDRESS$  = 43% &
250                                                                 REM
300 MAP (RECOUT) FULL_RECORD    = 80%
350                                                                 REM
400 PRINT FIRST_NAME$,LAST_NAME$
420 PRINT FULL_ADDRESS$
```

would result in:

```
RITA              JONES         S.
130 PINE ST       PITTSBURGH    PA 15261
```

The MAP statements refer to the same record, which contains 80 bytes of data.

III.E.3   Updating MAPped Values

Let's assume we have created a file named "STUDENT.DAT" and its records were defined by the MAP statements used in the above sections. It is to be a small file containing the names and addresses of a department's majors. A program is to be written that will permit someone working at a terminal to inspect the contents of each record and make any necessary changes. The resulting output, or new file, is to be called "STUDMST.DAT". The following steps are to be included in the program:

1. Lay out the records using MAP statements.
2. OPEN and define the files.
3. Get a record.
4. Inspect the record.
5. Make any changes.
6. Put the record.
7. Close the files.

The program might look like this:

```
100 MAP (RECOUT)    LAST_NAME$   =   20%  &
                  , FIRST_NAME$  =   15%  &
                  , INITIAL$     =    2%  &
                  , ADDRESS$     =   20%  &
                  , CITY$        =   15%  &
                  , STATE$       =    2%  &
                  , FILL$        =    1%  &
                  , ZIP$         =    5%
150                                                             REM
200 MAP (DATA_REC) FULL_NAME$    =   37%  &
                  , FULL_ADDRESS$=   53%  &
250                                                             REM
300 OPEN 'STUDENT.DAT'                         &
    FOR INPUT AS FILE #1                        &
  , MAP DATA_REC
350                                                             REM
400 OPEN 'STUDMST.DAT'                         &
        FOR OUTPUT AS FILE #2                   &
  , MAP DATA_REC
450 REM
452 REM *************************************
454 REM *                                     *
456 REM *     GET record from 1st file        *
458 REM *                                     *
460 REM *************************************
462 REM
500 GET #1
510 IF LAST_NAME$ = "END-OF-FILE" THEN 1400
600 PRINT FULL_NAME$
610 PRINT FULL_ADDRESS$
620 PRINT
630 INPUT "ANY CHANGES (NO, YES) ==> "; CHANGES$
640 PRINT
650 IF CHANGES$ = "NO" THEN 1300
660 REM
```

```
662 REM ****************************************
664 REM *                                      *
666 REM *     INPUT option for processing      *
668 REM *                                      *
670 REM ****************************************
672 REM
700 PRINT "   1 FULL NAME         5 FULL ADDRESS"
710 PRINT "   2 FIRST NAME        6 ADDRESS    "
720 PRINT "   3 INITIAL           7 CITY       "
730 PRINT "   4 LAST NAME         8 STATE      "
740 PRINT "                       9 ZIP        "
750 PRINT "   10 GO TO NEXT PERSON"
760 PRINT
770                                                          REM
780 INPUT "ENTER OPTION = = > "; OPT%
785 IF OPT% > 10 THEN 800
790 ON OPTION% GO TO 900,1000,1000,1000               &
          ,1100,1200,1200,1200,1200                   &
          ,1300
800 PRINT "INCORRECT OPTION"
810 LET ER% = ER% + 1
820 IF ER% < 3 THEN 780 ELSE                     &
      \ PRINT "PLEASE SEEK ASSISTANCE"            &
      \ PRINT "OR CHECK USER MANUAL"              &
      \ PRINT "BYE FOR NOW"                       &
      \ GOTO 1400
900 REM
902 REM *****************************************
904 REM *                                       *
906 REM *    900 = Change full name             *
908 REM *                                       *
910 REM *****************************************
912 REM
915 INPUT "FIRST NAME      = = > "; FIRST_NAME$
920 INPUT "INITIAL         = = > "; INITIAL$
930 INPUT "LAST NAME       = = > "; LAST_NAME$
940 GO TO 600
950 REM
```

```
952 REM **************************************
954 REM *                                    *
956 REM *    1000 = Change part of name      *
958 REM *                                    *
960 REM **************************************
962 REM
1000 IF OPT% = 2 THEN INPUT "FIRST NAME = => " ; FIRST_NAME$   &
     \ GOTO 600                                                &
     ELSE IF OPT% = 3 THEN INPUT "INITIAL = => "; INITIAL$     &
     \ GOTO 600                                                &
     ELSE IF OPT% = 4 THEN INPUT "LAST NAME = => "; LAST_NAME$ &
     \ GOTO 600
1050 REM
1052 REM **************************************
1054 REM *                                    *
1056 REM *    1100 = Change full address      *
1058 REM *                                    *
1060 REM **************************************
1062
1100 INPUT "ADDRESS     = => "; ADDRESS$
1120 INPUT "CITY        = => "; CITY$
1130 INPUT "STATE (AA)  = => "; STATE$
1140 INPUT "ZIP         = => "; ZIP$
1150 GO TO 600
1200 REM
1202 REM **************************************
1204 REM *                                    *
1206 REM *    1200 = Change part of name      *
1208 REM *                                    *
1210 REM **************************************
1210 REM
1215 IF OPT% - 6 THEN INPUT "ADDRESS = => "; ADDRESS$          &
     \ GOTO 600                                                &
     ELSE IF OPT% = 7 THEN INPUT "CITY = => "; CITY$           &
     \ GOTO 600                                                &
     ELSE IF OPT% = 8 THEN INPUT "STATE (AA) = => "; STATE$    &
     \ GOTO 600                                                &
     ELSE IF OPT% = 9 THEN INPUT "ZIP = => "; ZIP$             &
     \ GOTO 600
1300 REM
```

```
1302 REM ******************************************
1304 REM *                                        *
1306 REM *    PUT new record to 2nd file          *
1308 REM *                                        *
1310 REM ******************************************
1312 REM
1315 PUT # 1
1320 GO TO 500
1350                                            REM
1400 CLOSE # 1
1500 END
```

III.F   REVIEW QUESTIONS

1. Explain the formats of the following varaiables:

   ARC   ARC$ ARC%

2. What are variables and constants? Why are variables necessary if programs are to work effectively? How are variable
   names constructed? List a set of general guidelines for constructing variable names.
3. What does the phrase "program maintenance" mean? How
   can programs be designed to ease maintenance efforts? Will
   extra initial effort repay itself in the end? In what ways?
4. How are record layouts used? What is their purpose?
5. Explain the parallel between a record layout and a MAP
   statement. What does a MAP statement actually do? Why
   are variables assigned in MAP statements considered to be
   static and not *dynamic*?
6. How are multiple MAPs constructed? In what ways can
   MAP statements ease program development and maintenance?

III.G   EXERCISES

1. Write a MAP statement from the following record layout:

VARIABLE NAME	DATA TYPE	DATA SIZE	CONTENTS
ID_NUMBER	N	9	Use soc-sec number
LAST_NAME	A	20	
FIRST_NAME	A	10	
MIDDLE_INITIAL	A	2	One chr. + '.'
ADDRESS	A	20	Street address
CITY	A	12	
STATE	A	2	Use P O Standard
ZIP	N	5	

Lay out an 80-character key punch card for input.

2. Divide the above into two logical groups, and write multiple MAP statements for them.

3. Write a program to INPUT the data items MAPped in 1 above. If a data item is entered in a different order, will the program still work? Why or why not?

4. Modify the above exercise so that the data may be changed from the terminal.

5. Prepare and run a program for a small company that maintains video games. First, design a record layout to include an id-number, name, type of game, manufacturer, cost (9,999.99), and skill level (advanced, intermediate, beginning). Then write a progam that will display upon request either the id-number, type of game, and manufacturer, or the name, skill level, and cost. The program should also include a section to update the cost. [For this exercise, MAP statements are not required. It might be best at this point to consider using an array to store the data. A READ..DATA statement can be used to store the data in an array, and the results can be printed on hard copy.]

IV

Files, Records, and Data Storage

IV.A   FILE AND DATA MANAGEMENT

ADVANCED BASIC has in the main to do with data management, and with systems design and development.   As soon as BASIC programming goes beyond games and single program applications, the programmer is faced with analyzing, collecting, coding, storing, retrieving, and updating data.   Improper data management will produce not only incorrect results, but also chaos. Put quite simply, an ability to manage data properly and accurately is an absolute necessity for those wishing to become system analysts and project managers.

It is, in fact, an ability that is necessary for anyone wishing to install and operate any form of data or information system.   If the sales figures for microcomputers are accurate indicators, there is an ever-increasing need for data systems knowledge across a wide spread of computer owners. And if these new owners are to plan, develop, and use their microsystems for something other than hobby interests and limited programming, then they, too, will at some point be confronted with managing and controlling their data.

In this chapter, the basic concepts of data storage and file definition are examined. Attention is also given error and debugging routines.

IV.B FILE HIERARCHY: PHYSICAL VS. LOGICAL

Traditionally, files are said to consist of one or more records, which are, in turn, made up of one or more fields. Fields are formed by one or more characters, or data items. This delineation often mixes levels. Only characters exist in reality. *They are physically real and take up space*, whether written on paper, punched into a computer card, or stored magnetically on a disk or diskette.

On the other hand, to consider a string of characters—the record—as being composed of fields is a logical consideration. *Records are defined for logical purposes.* Whether a character within a given string belongs to one field or to another depends upon how one views the string. There is nothing absolute about a field or, for that matter, a record—unless, of course, the file consists of only one character.

IV.B.1 Physical: Files, Blocks, and Characters

The focal point of a data system is the file, or a set of files. Files are composed physically of characters, and are stored on peripheral devices, such as diskettes, disks, disk packs, and magnetic tapes. The act of moving characters to a file from the computer's memory, or of retrieving characters from a file, is part of the computer's overall operating system.

This operating system groups characters into physical strings called BLOCKS. A block is defined here as the number of characters that is transferred in a single read or write operation. The operating system stores characters in storage areas called BUFFERS; and when a buffer is filled, a block of data is written to the storage device. On many disk systems, a block consists of 512 characters.

On magnetic tape, the size can become quite large, but since most BASIC systems are disk oriented, emphasis is given data blocked for storage on disks or diskettes.

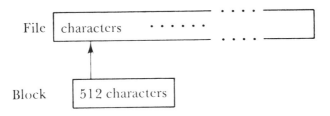

IV.B.1.a   File Selection: OPEN/CLOSE

Before files can be created or accessed, they must first be OPENed for processing. In this step, the system is told which file(s) is to be processed, and in what manner.

If the file does not yet exist—i.e., it is a new file and needs to be created—the file is opened for OUTPUT. No matter what other process is to be performed, if the file already exists, it is opened for INPUT.

Once processing is complete, a file must be CLOSEd before termination of the program. If this step is not taken, no one can guarantee that the integrity of the file will be maintained.

```
ln  OPEN 'file-name' [FOR INPUT, OUTPUT] AS FILE #n
    .
    .
    .
ln  CLOSE #n

100 OPEN 'IS100.DAT' FOR OUTPUT AS FILE #1
    .
    .
999 CLOSE #1

[ ] = optional choice
```

In this example, a file to be named 'IS200.DAT' is to be created. Note the single quotes delimiting the file name. It will be a sequential file by default because no other organizational technique is given.

> The file is opened for output because a file with the same name should *not* already exist. If there should, however, already be a file with the same name, the previous contents of the file will not be accessed.

If no generation is given, then a new file is created with a new generation number (old number + 1), but the contents of the original file will not be available for processing.

'AS FILE #n' indicates the number by which the file will be referenced throughout the program. Even though a file name must be given in the OPEN statement, it is not used elsewhere in the program. The pound sign (#) plus a number becomes the "name" for the file within the program. This is called a CHANNEL NUMBER. This convention may seem strange at first, but consider the following.

```
100 INPUT "NAME OF FILE ";FILE_NAME$
200 OPEN FILE_NAME$ FOR OUTPUT AS FILE #1
```

This format permits a program to create different data files without making changes to the program. The name of the file is input from the terminal, and all output is then stored under this name. The program, however, uses the same channel number each time it is run.

If a file already exists (with a unique name), its contents may be accessed using 'FOR INPUT':

```
100 OPEN 'IS200.DAT' FOR INPUT AS FILE #1
        .
        .
        .
999 CLOSE #1
```

IV.B.1.b Filetype: ORGANIZATION

The various options are discussed in the following under FILE ORGANIZATION and under RECORD LENGTHS. At this point, one example will be sufficient. Note the format and the use of this statement so that other options may be added.

If the organization clause is omitted, BASIC assumes the file to be sequential and the record length to be variable. This is the same as if the following clause had been included in the program.

```
100 OPEN 'IS200.DAT' FOR OUTPUT AS FILE #1   &
        , ORGANIZATION SEQUENTIAL VARIABLE
```

& = line continuation. The next line does not have a number.
, = a separator. It is used at beginning of each option.

IV.B.1.c File Operations: ACCESS

When ACCESS is used as an attribute for the OPEN statement, only certain operations may be performed on the file.

```
100 OPEN 'IS200.DAT' FOR INPUT AS FILE #1     &
        ,ORGANIZATION SEQUENTIAL VARIABLE     &
        ,ACCESS READ
```

In this example, an existing file is opened for reading only. The contents of the file will be protected from any inadvertent changes, either by rewriting or by updating operations.   Other options include:

> APPEND
> MODIFY
> SCRATCH
> WRITE

IV.B.1.d   File Definition: TEMPORARY

When TEMPORARY is included in the OPEN statement, the file is deleted from the system when it is closed. This option permits the creation of work files for intermediate storage during program execution.

IV.B.1.e   Logical: Files, Records, Fields, and Characters

The programmer determines record formats, record sizes, and the organizational method used in creating the file. Logically, a file is a collection of related data. Once a block of data is in core memory, it is considered logically to be divided into units of characters, called records.   For one reason or another, characters within a record belong to each other. Records themselves may be further logically defined as consisting of fields of characters. A record is conversely a grouping of one or more fields; and a block is physically made up of one or more records. In some rare instances, a record may be so large that it spans several blocks.

On a disk system, the size of the blocks is usually fixed; they are quite often 512 characters in length. Since this means that 512 characters are read or written at a time, a multiple of strings of characters which are less than 512 characters in length will result in blank spaces being written to the disk.

For example, if a record is defined to contain 80 characters, then six records can be written at one write to disk storage:

$$32 = 512 - (6 * 80)$$

with the result that the last 32 characters of the block contain blanks. The less blanks, the more efficient the use of the storage system,

File | Amy   92 88Bill   88 87Carl   100 93   · · · · ·

Records | Amy   92 88   Carl   100 93

Fields   92   Carl

Characters   9   a

especially whenever logical sizes can be determined with regard to actual physical space.

It is important to note that on many computer systems, once a file is defined and created, all subsequent references to this file must match this definition. Failure to do so will result in system I/O errors and an abnormal termination of the program.

IV.B.2   Record Lengths

If a blank computer card is put into a card-reader and its contents copied and stored in the computer's internal memory, 80 blank characters arc stored. Should additional cards be read, a record will be created for each card, and each record will be exactly 80 characters long. Should the cards contain punched data, 80 characters (including the trailing blanks to the end of the card) would still be stored in the record. No matter how much of the card is used to contain punched data, all the records will be the same length.

But records do not always have to be the same length. In fact, saving blanks often wastes space. Trailing blanks are, therefore, often stripped from the end of the last piece of punched data to the end of the card. When this happens, the resulting records will not be the same length.

Since records are usually blocked before storage on external devices, it is possible when records are of varying lengths that one block will contain more records than another block. When moving records to a block, it is a simple matter of mathematics to know if there is enough space remaining to hold the next record. A block is set to hold *n* number of characters, and each record moved to the block takes up a certain number of characters.

When blocks are retrieved, then matters look different. Unless the records stored within the block are all the same length, the computer will have to somehow know where each record begins and ends. Record formats are thus usually divided into two primary groupings (fixed vs. variable length) and this information stored in the file directory.

IV.B.2.a   Fixed-Length Records: RECORDSIZE

When records are always the same length, they are termed FIXED-LENGTH records. As records are moved to the buffer, their length will be checked. If they are shorter than prescribed, they are padded with blanks. And on many systems, if they are longer than the predetermined length, they are truncated—or at best an error situation occurs.

Records are moved to the buffer sequentially until there is no longer enough space for another complete record. If space remains in the buffer, it will then be filled with blanks before the contents of the buffer are written to storage.

BUFFER
(Block = 512)

Record (100)	Record (100)	Record (100)	Record (100)	Record (100)	12 spaces

Fixed-length records require less overhead than variable-length records, but there always exists the possibility of wasted space at the end of each record as well as at the end of each block. Much of this waste can be eliminated with a little thought and planning.

There are times when fixed length records are needed. The following should, however, be used with discretion to assure that space is not wasted.

The RECORDSIZE clause sets a predetermined length for each record. If the data is shorter then the recordsize, it will be padded with blanks to fill the record. If it is longer, it will be truncated to fit the record, and data could be lost.

```
100 OPEN 'IS200.DAT' FOR OUTPUT AS FILE #1        &
        ,ORGANIZATION IS SEQUENTIAL               &
        ,RECORDSIZE = 80%
200 LINPUT "NAME & ADDRESS > ";NAME__ADDR$
210 PRINT #1, NAME__ADDR$
```

I.V.B.2.b   Variable-Length Records:
TERMINAL FORMAT

Variable-length records may be of any length up to the maximum
record size established for the file. The length of each record is
calculated and the result added to the beginning of each record as
it is stored.

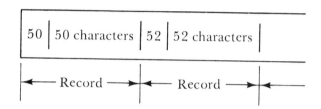

`, ORGANIZATION SEQUENTIAL VARIABLE`

Once variable length is specified as the record format, the system
handles blocking and deblocking. Variable-length records make
efficient use of storage space, but the system will use more overhead
as it processes the records.

TERMINAL-FORMAT indicates that the records are not of
any fixed length. They usually contain a single member or a single
string, and the maximum length is usually some default of numbers of characters. A file composed of terminal format records is
analogous to a file made up of DATA statements, but without line
numbers and the verb DATA. Instead of data existing between
commas, they exist in records. This format is certainly not the
most efficient for a data and information system, but it is commonly
found on smaller systems.

```
100 OPEN 'IS200.DAT;2' FOR INPUT AS FILE #1      &
          , ORGANIZATION SEQUENTIAL              &
          , ACCESS READ
200 OPEN 'IS200.DAT;3' FOR OUTPUT AS FILE #2
      .
      .
      .
300 FOR X = 1 TO 25
310     INPUT #1; NAME$, GRADE
320        IF GRADE = 999 THEN 400
330        IF GRADE > 90 THEN 350
340     PRINT #2; NAME$
350 NEXT X
400   .
      .
999 CLOSE #1, CLOSE #2
```

This program searches the first 25 records of file #1 and writes to file #2 the names of those students with a grade of 91 or better. Should a last record be reached (grade = 999), then the search is terminated.

As is indicated above, there are better ways to process and handle data, but this is a beginning point, which works well enough for many operations.

IV.B.2.c General Format

```
ln OPEN 'FILE-NAME' [ FOR INPUT ]  AS FILE #n
                    [ FOR OUTPUT ]
          [, [ORGANIZATION] SEQUENTIAL [FIXED      ] ]
                                       [VARIABLE    ]
          [, RECORDSIZE = n%]
          [, ACCESS [READ     ] ]
                    [APPEND    ]
                    [MODIFY    ]
                    [SCRATCH   ]
                    [WRITE     ]
          [, TEMPORARY]
```

IV.B.3 Files, Records, and Programmers

It is important for people writing programs for interaction with files to remember that to the operating system characters and files are physical entities, while they, the programmers, may be viewing the data quite differently. One represents a physical organization of real data, while the other presents a logical understanding of the same data. And while this book deals with data which is by all means logically related, the physical aspects of these same data will from time to time have to be taken into account.

IV.C FILE ORGANIZATION

The basic logical unit of the file is the record. FILE ORGANIZATION is the manner in which records are *considered* to be stored in the file. There are four primary file organization techniques:

SEQUENTIAL
RELATIVE
BLOCK I/O
INDEXED

and one of these is used to store, find, retrieve, and update records. The term *considered* is used here because modern record management systems quite often manage characters and records in only one, very efficient manner. Yet for programming reasons, file organization techniques are maintained for logical planning and data system management.

If no specific organization is selected in the program, BASIC assumes the file to be organized sequentially. Once a file is created using one of the organization techniques, it should always be processed using that same technique. This does not mean that it is not possible to change processing techniques, but such changes tend to become messy. Whenever possible, it is best to carefully select one of the organizational techniques, and then stick with it.

Each individual organizational method will be discussed separately in later chapters. The following paragraphs can be read as an introduction to file types, with details reserved for later.

IV.C.1 Sequential Files

A sequential file contains records that are logically considered to be stored in the order in which they were written. The file is said to be processed from top to bottom, or "first in—first out" (FIFO).

```
Record 1  | characters   · · ·
Record 2  | characters   · · ·
Record 3  | characters   · · ·
          |      ·
          |      ·
          |      ·
Record n  | characters   · · ·
```

The first record written will become record #1 and will be the first record read; the second record written will be record #2 and will be the second record read; etc. If new records are later added to a sequential file, they are *appended* to the file—i.e., they are added at the bottom of the file. Sequential files work well on almost any storage device.

Sequential files are processed from beginning to end and are, therefore, best used when each record in the file is to be processed in the order in which it was stored. An example of such a file would be an address listing, used to print mailing labels. Sequential files require a large amount of processing to delete or update records. Usually the whole file must be read and examined, and a new file created. For this reason, sequential files are most often found in batch-oriented systems. They are not used as often in data and information systems.

IV.C.2   Relative Files

A RELATIVE FILE can be imagined to contain a series of boxes, or cells. Each box contains one record, and they are numbered consecutively from one to however many boxes are needed. Each record is then assigned a number from one to n, according to its position relative to the beginning of the file.

Record 1	Record 2	Record 3	Record 4	$\cdots$	Record n
Box 1	Box 2	Box 3	Box 4		Box n

Records are written or retrieved by box number (a record's relative position), or sequentially by omitting box numbers.

If an inventory system, for example, contains 100 or less items, then each item is assigned a number between 1 and 100. This number also becomes the box number in which data about the inventory item will be stored, and from which it will be retrieved. Data on inventory item #4 will be found in box #4, data on item #10 in box #10, etc.

Relative files are extremely efficient in terms of speed and use of storage space. The system simply goes directly to the box (record storage area) without a great amount of system overhead. Each file is numerically relative to some beginning address, and since mathematical calculations are done internally, I/O is limited to a few basic operations. Relative files reside on disk devices.

They are best used for accessing records randomly and for operations in which a key or item number can be equated or con-verted to a relative record (box) number. Relative files are easy to process, and data can be quickly retrieved, updated, and stored. Since it is almost always necessary to state the expected total num-ber of boxes in advance, boxes that are never used (overestimated) waste space. Again, on many modern record management systems, this is not always true, and relative files are best used when their organization offers benefits to the programmer and the application being developed.

IV.C.3   Block I/0

BLOCK I/O files are much the same as relative files, except that more than one record is stored in each box, or cell. Data records are, therefore, blocked, and each block of records is then written or read as needed. Block I/O files permit very efficient use of disk (especially diskette) space.

IV.C.4   Indexed Files

INDEXED FILES have at least two components. They contain an index to the location (address) of the data records, and they contain the data records themselves. For this to happen, each data record must contain at least one *unique key*, the primary key. This key must be a field within the record and is used to store and retrieve the record. The index contains a copy of the key and the location (address) on the disk of the record.

```
            INDEX                    •      RECORD

       Key        Address              Key Field

    ┌─────────┬──────────┐       ┌──────────────── · · · ──────┐
    │  14732  │ 1007345  │       │  .. 14732 .....      · · ·   │
    │  14967  │ 1007862  │       └──────────────────── · · · ──┘
    │  16827  │ 0083154  │       ┌─────────────── · · · ───────┐
    └─────────┴──────────┘       │  .. 16827 .....              │
                                 └───────────── · · · ──────────┘
                                 ┌────────────── · · · ─────────┐
                                 │  .. 14967 .....              │
                                 └──────────────── · · · ───────┘
```

ALTERNATE KEYS, or secondary keys, may also be assigned so that records may be retrieved using several different options. Indexed files can, therefore, be processed in more than one way, including sequentially without keys, by primary key, or secondary key or by a combination of keys. These files are more flexible when retrieving records because they can be searched using more than one key. These keys, however, must be a field within the records, and the processing of the keys does require more system overhead than other storage options.

IV.D   RECORD MANAGEMENT SYSTEMS

The four file organization techniques outlined above will be discussed in further detail in this and in following chapters.   But suppose—for the sake of another possibility—that a disk system permits only one(!) storage method. In this system, logical divisions of a file, considered to be the record, are stored, searched for, and retrieved in a manner permitting maximum utilization of disk space, as well as greater speed over an average group of users.

The user's program supplies the system with a chunk of data, which is logical in content as far as the user is concerned. It is, however, strictly physical as far as the disk is concerned. The program may or may not also supply a unique key, which may or may not be a field within the record.

If no unique key is passed by the program along with the data, the system creates its own keys (1, 2, 3, etc.) and then stores the data where space is available. Addresses (and system-user created) keys are then stored in a index. If no unique key is passed, but each record is relative to some beginning point, then the relative factor becomes the key, and the process continues. And if a unique key is passed, then the system proceeds, using the new key.

This system has in concept a single storage system, with the advantage that records from logical sequential and relative files need not be in whole or in part stored continuously on the disk—and the disadvantage that indices must be maintained for the files. But with minicomputers having somewhere between 4k and 8k of internal memory, processing instructions at 6 to 8 MIPS (Million Instructions Per Second) and bus lines ferrying data at tremendous speeds, the trade-off is now in favor of disk storage space, which is usually at a premium. And if a program calls for secondary keys, the system will quickly retrieve and sort the needed fields, and create the needed index. The index, once created, will then also be stored, should it be needed again; but since secondary keys are not statistically used that often, the system can afford a little overhead from time to time for the sake of better space utilization.

Now, no system operates just like this; but many systems come close to it. Sequential, relative, and indexed files are historically conditioned. They present several very useful approaches to the logical organization of data. Be prepared, however, for some strange new possibilities. For example, it is often stated that individual records in a sequential file cannot be updated without making an entirely new copy of the file. In the system described above, updates would be possible by simply searching the file sequentially using the index until a key field in a record is found. The result would be an updated record without recopying and matching an entire file. If records most likely to be changed were periodically sorted to the beginning of the sequential file, there would be some overhead, but for single users on larger systems, the over-

head would be manageable. Additions would need to be appended
to the index even if one of the keys had earlier been deleted, but
only for logical considerations.

Because of this and other possibilities, it is always a good idea
to scan operating manuals, not for bothersome details, but for a
general understanding of how a disk system really does store, find,
and retrieve logical units, such as a record.

IV.E   FILE NAMES

Each file, no matter what the organization, must be given a *unique*
name. System rules may vary, but the need for uniqueness remains.
A name, which is in some respect different from all other names,
permits the system to create an index of file names and then to
store information about that file.

A systemwide convention—enforced for everyone—makes
life easier for system programmers and for everyone else in
general. The convention used here gives a file NAME, a possible
EXTENSION, and an optional GENERATION NUMBER.

NAME. ext; n

NAME (from 1 to 9 characters)

  ext (optional: from 1 to 3 characters)

    n (optional: a positive integer)

      ACCOUNTS.DAT;3

                        (Third generation of a
                          data file called ACCOUNTS)

      ACCOUNTS.BAS

                        (First generation of a BASIC
                          file called ACCOUNTS)

      ACCOUNTS

                        (First generation of file
                          called ACCOUNTS)

The logical aspects of the above names are obvious. Good file names which have meaning make life a whole lot easier for programmers and analysts. They mean little to the system itself, except that they must in some aspect be unique. Here, ACCOUNTS by itself has some, but restricted, meaning. The other examples are better because they give an indication of the contents of the file. One contains a program written in BASIC, and the other the data.

```
GRDIS.BAS     SEC1.DAT     IS2.DAT
IS3.DAT       IS4.DAT
```

On some systems, generations are not indicated numerically. Rather, a BACKUP file is created. Thus

```
ACCOUNTS.BAS
```

becomes

```
ACCOUNTS.BAK
```

whenever the former is updated. Unless backup files are specifically RENAMEd, a further update may cause their contents to be deleted:

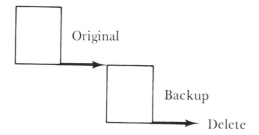

Original

Backup

Delete

IV.F   DATA FILES AND PROGRAM FILES

Files contain characters, and characters are used by humans both to write programs and to store data. An accounts receivable file is composed of data characters about certain accounts. Such files are called DATA FILES. Program statements written in BASIC are also stored in files. Usually one program is stored in one file; thus the name PROGRAM FILES.

While the computer views both types of files in the same manner when they are created, stored, retrieved, or updated, humans generally view these two types differently. BASIC statements are stored in files so they may be used to process data stored in other files.

IV.F.1　Program Files

In a data and information system, a BASIC program file—once it is created and accepted as containing a usable program—remains fairly stable. Relatively few changes are made to it. A BASIC program used to post accounts may be used over and over again, sometimes every working day for months, without changes. For this reason, BASIC programs are quite often compiled— i.e., rewritten in machine language, and stored to increase system efficiency. This practice results in two sets of programs for a data and information system: source and object programs.

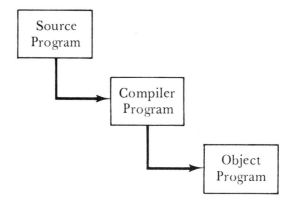

On some systems, it is also necessary to LINK the object programs. The result is an executable module. It is this module that is RUN by the system. It contains the object code and any system instructions necessary to completely run the program— i.e., instructions for using a particular printer, model of disk drive, etc. The actual result is a third program, or module.

Source programs and object programs are generally stored separately, and copies are made of each should disaster or human error result in the loss of a current program. Source programs are often stored off-line, while object (linked) programs are kept online—ready to run each day.

When the above practice is used, routines are written to copy groups of programs into a PROGRAM LIBRARY. With one command, libraries (or groups of programs) can be easily stored or retrieved. In computer terms, BASIC programs are stored in pro-

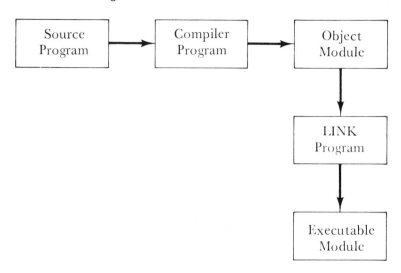

gram libraries, and compiled versions of these programs are stored in object (link) libraries.

IV.F.2   Data Files   System Charts

DATA files contain data for processing by programs. Data files must also be copied and protected. If a data and information system were to lose its data files, it would be rendered helpless. Almost every data and information system includes provisions for BACKUP of its activities. Loss of data is not only disastrous; it is, in reality, inexcusable.

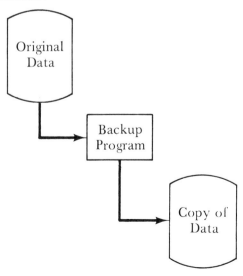

Computer vendors provide specialized routines and procedures to protect data files. No data or information process can be said to be complete until proper BACKUPS have been created.

For data files, whose contents change almost daily, a generation system is used. The data file retains its unique name, but the generation number changes each time the file is processed. This is especially true for master files.

ACCOUNT SYSTEM CHART

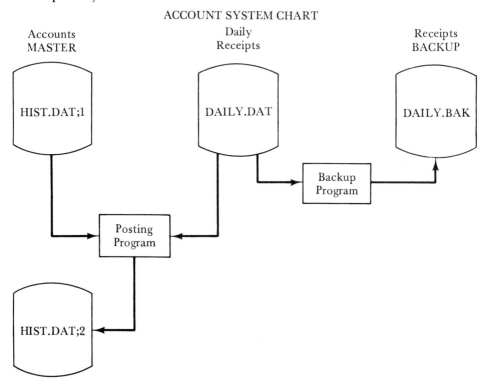

In the above system chart, the daily receipts are first copied to a backup file, using the backup program. If something should happen during posting, then a copy of the original daily receipts will be available. HIST.DAT;1 as the original master file will be used as input to the posting program. Should something happen to this file, one presumes there is a version-0 somewhere. After the posting run, then generation 2 (HIST.DAT;2) will be tomorrow's input, and generation 1 (HIST.DAT;1) is history. Tomorrow's output will result in generation 3, etc. In such a system, if at some point something should fail or if there should be bad data or program error, there will be a RESTARTING point.

The above system has four program files and four data files: two BASIC source files, two object files, two data files (master and translation), one backup file, and one new master file. Each type must be carefully planned and protected. In a data and information system, there are only a few files that are totally static over a period of time, and there are also only a few files that can be easily and inexpensively recreated.

IV.G ERROR ROUTINES

Error handling routines are provided in BASIC to ensure data and file integrity. This does not mean that everytime BASIC detects an "error" something bad has happened. Actually, error routines can be used positively to edit data as well as simply to detect an end-of-file, eliminating the need for dummy records at the end of each file. For the programmer, this feature of BASIC offers editorial tools for data control and management. For the system, it offers greater flexibility and helps reduce the error margin.

The following paragraphs should be carefully studied. The inclusion of error trapping routines in data and information systems is an absolute necessity. Not only does their proper use help ensure continued successful operation of a system, but also they can serve as one additional tool to provide better user-oriented procedures.

IV.G.1 General Format: ON ERROR GOTO/RESUME

When BASIC is confronted with a file or data error during execution, it normally will terminate the program after sending an error message to the terminal. This can be frustrating, especially if the error could have been corrected easily and execution continued. It is also sometimes desirable to take remedial action or to branch to another program module when an error situation occurs.

If an ON ERROR GOTO statement is included very early in the program, BASIC transfers control to the line number specified. This will occur whenever an error is encountered.

```
ln ON ERROR GOTO n

10 ON ERROR GOTO 19000
   .
   .
   .
19000 (resume here)
```

Whenever an error is encountered after line 10 in the program, control is transferred to line 19000 (this number is usually used even though the program might contain larger line numbers). Here the program can be RESUMED, and the error situation evaluated.

Suppose that after all data in a file had been processed, totals remained to be printed before program termination. Unless the exact amount of data were known before hand, or unless dummy data were appended as a last record, the program would eventually try to read past the end-of-file. An error situation would occur, the program would be terminated, and the totals would not be printed. The following program, however, handles this situation.

```
100 ON ERROR GOTO 19000
200 OPEN 'IS200.DAT' FOR INPUT AS FILE #1   &
              , ACCESS READ
300 INPUT #1; INCOMING_DATA$
400 PRINT INCOMING_DATA$
500 LET TOTAL_RECORDS = TOTAL_RECORDS + 1
600 GOTO 300
       .
       .
       .
800 PRINT "END OF FILE: "; TOTAL_RECORDS; " TOTAL RECORDS"
900 GOTO 20000
       .
       .
       .
19000 RESUME 800
20000 CLOSE #1
20100 END
```

The loop between 300 and 600 will be processed until an attempt is made in line 300 to read past the end-of-file. This causes an error situation, and control is automatically passed to line 19000, where the program is resumed at line 800. Note that line 19000 contains only the verb RESUME and a line number. Actually processing begins again at the indicated line number. Error routines can also be used to edit data. In the following example, the program is continued even when an incorrect data format has been entered from the terminal.

```
100 ON ERROR GOTO 19000
200 OPEN . . . . . .
300 INPUT "NAME and GRADE "; NAME$, GRADE
400     IF NAME$ = "END" THEN . . . .
500     PRINT #1, NAME$, GRADE
600 GOTO 300
       .
       .
       .
800 PRINT "NOT A GRADE " \ GOTO 300
       .
       .
       .
19000 RESUME 800
       .
       .
       .
```

In this example, should a letter of the alphabet be inadvertently entered in 300, the program would not be terminated. Rather, control would be transferred to line 19000, an error message displayed, and execution continued.

IV.G.2   Error Line Number: ERL

The program just cited assumes, however, that the only possible error could be incorrect data entry. This would not necessarily be the case. It might be that for some reason a file could not be opened or, for that matter, closed. It is, therefore, helpful to know in which line the error occurred. This is done through the built-in function ERL. When used, it returns the line number in which the error was encountered.

```
.
.
.
19000 IF (ERL = 400) THEN PRINT "INCORRECT DATA" \ RESUME  &
            ELSE ON ERROR GOTO 0
.
.
.
```

Should the error not have occurred in line 400, then the program will be terminated; otherwise the error message will be displayed and the program resumed.

ON ERROR GOTO 0 returns error handling to the system. The BASIC program is terminated, and proper action, including display of error messages, undertaken. This statement assures an orderly shutdown of the run. Nonetheless, it is usually best to handle as many errors as possible within the program. This gives the programmer a greater degree of control over the data system itself. The inclusion of this statement should not simply default any errors to system programs; it is included to catch unanticipated errors. The program should be prepared to handle specific, possible errors. Unexpected errors are then left to the system.

I.V.G.3   Error Number: ERR

The above example still does not indicate *what* error occured in line 400. This is done by checking the actual run-time error number. BASIC uses the built-in function ERR to obtain the system number for errors as it encounters them.

```
19000 IF (ERL = 400) AND (ERR = 50)                      &
            THEN PRINT "NOT A GRADE"  RESUME             &
            ELSE RESUME 20000
```

Error number 50 signals a data format error. Should any other error occur at line 400, the program would be terminated.

Actual error numbers (and messages) are found in user manuals, usually under "RUN-TIME ERROR MESSAGES". Possible error numbers and texts will also be found as needed in the following chapters.

IV.G.4   ERROR TEXT: ERT$

It is possible to simply let BASIC print the appropriate error message. It does this by retrieving the error message from the system and then displaying it as requested. When combined with the error number, the built-in function ERT$ will contain the error message.

```
19000 IF  (ERR = 400)  AND  (ERR = 50)               &
          THEN PRINT ERT$ (50) \ RESUME             &
          ELSE RESUME 20000
```

The text for error number 50 will be printed on the terminal (or in the run log) before resuming a line 400 or termination.

IV.H   PROGRAM SAMPLE

    I. Input (disk)

        A. File name: IS200.DAT;2
        B. Recordsize Fixed/80 (from cards)
        C. Fields   NAME$,GRD1,GRD2,GRD3,GRD4

    II. Process

      $AVG = INT((GRD1 + GRD2 + GRD3 + GRD4)/4 + .5)$

    III. Output (printer)

```
NAME$    AVG

NAME$    Error messages
*********************************************************
*                                                       *
*             RUN-TIME ERRORS                           *
*                                                       *
*    2 = Illegal file name                              *
*    5 = Cannot find file                               *
*   11 = End of file                                    *
*   52 = Illegal number                                 *
*   59 = Not enough data in record                      *
*                                                       *
*********************************************************
```

```
100 ON ERROR GOTO 19000
200 INPUT "File to be processed ";FIL$
300 OPEN FIL$ FOR INPUT AS FILE #1
350                                                          REM
400 INPUT #1;NAME$,GRD1'GRD2'GRD3'GRD4
500    AVG = INT((GRD1 + GRD2 + GRD3 + GRD4)/4 + .5)
600    PRINT NAME$,AVG
700 GOTO 400
800                                                          REM
19000 IF (ERL=300) AND  (ERR=2)   THEN PRINT ERT$(ERR)       &
          \ RESUME  300      ELSE                            &
       IF (ERL=300) AND  (ERR=5)   THEN PRINT ERT$(ERR)      &
          \ RESUME  20100    ELSE                            &
       IF (ERL=400) AND  (ERR=52)  THEN PRINT NAME$,ERT$(ERR) &
          \ RESUME  400      ELSE                            &
       IF (ERL=400) AND  (ERR=59)  THEN PRINT NAME$,ERT$(ERR) &
          \ RESUME  400      ELSE                            &
       IF (ERL=400) AND  (ERR=11)  THEN RESUME 20000         &
                          ELSE ON  ERROR GOTO 0
19100                                                        REM
20000 CLOSE #1
20100 END
```

IV. Input Data

```
ABLE,100,92,93,94
BAKER,75,82,79,83
CHARLEY,92,88,9U,85
DOLLY,93,92,88
EMILY,93,94,89,96
```

V. Output Data

```
ABLE        95
BAKER       80
CHARLEY     Illegal number
DOLLY       Not enough data in record
EMILY       93
```

IV.I REVIEW QUESTIONS

1. Using the common delineation for data files:

File - Record - Field - Character

explain which are considered physical and which logical. Can a field and a record ever be physically the same? How many characters must a field have? Could there ever be a "null" file?

2. What does the OPEN statement in BASIC do? Why is it necessary when data files are being processed?

3. What is an input buffer? An output buffer? How do buffers relate to blocks of data? Are buffers considered physical or logical?

4. How are records, blocks, and files related?

5. Explain the similarities and the differences among sequential, relative, and indexed files. How are relative and block I/O files related? What is a backup file, and why do backup files exist?

6. Explain the use of primary and secondary keys. Would there be any purpose in designing secondary keys for relative files? How are the keys for indexed and relative files different?

7. What is a program file? How is it different from a data file? Can your computer system recognize the difference?

8. What are source modules, object modules, and executable modules? Why are they sometimes stored in program libraries?

9. What are "error" routines? How can they be used as a programming tool?

10. Where can one find the BASIC error codes and messages in your center?

IV.J EXERCISES

1. Using the sample program at the end of the chapter as a guide, prepare and run a similar program on your system. Be sure to check and test each error code.

2. a. Draw a system chart for a small inventory system, which is to be updated once a day. Include all backup files.

   b. Then create a record layout for the data items in each file.

   c. And, finally, prepare a MAP statement for each of the records.

3. Draw a diagram illustrating how the master file in 2a might look logically for each of the following:

a. Sequential file

b. Relative file

c. Block I/O file

d. Indexed file

V

Sequential Files

V.A SEQUENTIAL FILE PROCESSING

This chapter presents a review of sequential file processing. It also introduces two of the more traditional uses of sequential files: magnetic tape files and batch processing.

Sequential files contain records stored in the order in which they were created. No matter how the system may handle these records, they are considered by the programmer to be contiguous. The first record written to the file is followed by the second, then the third, then the fourth, and so on. In the same manner, records read from a sequential file will be read in the order in which they were created: first, second, third, etc. New records are appended to the end of the file.

Sequential files are a viable option when data is believed to be correct and basically constant over a period of time. Sequential files should also be considered when large chunks of the data are to be retrieved and processed in a predictable order. But once there is a need to make frequent, sporadic changes to data, or to retrieve a single record deep in the file, sequential file processing can become costly in time and efficiency.

This does not mean that sequential files should never be processed interactively. Batch operations are considered in detail in this chapter because sequential files lend themselves to batch processing. Note, however, the number of BASIC statements that can be used in programs accessing sequential files from a terminal. It is a matter of considering the file size and the predictable location of the record needed and, to some extent, of anticipating the type of operations to be performed.

V.A.1   Current-Record and Next-Record Pointers

As records are processed, the system keeps track of which record is being processed at any given time. In computer terminology, a *record pointer* indicates which record is the "current" record. This wording means that the system has a routine for processing records that keeps notes on the location of the record currently being processed, both in its internal memory and on a storage device. For sequential files, the "next" record is logically the one following the current record. Physical location is left to the system and its manner of handling files.

V.A.2   Sequential File Operations

Once data is entered into the system, examined, and coded, it can be stored for later reference. For sequential files, this means storing and retrieving logically in sequential order, from first to last (FIFO). The commands PUT, APPEND, FIND, GET, UPDATE, and SCRATCH are used in BASIC to move data from working areas, to buffers, to storage media, and back again. These commands give control over data movement to the programmer. They are also introduced here in anticipation of the many data formatting possibilities in the next chapter.

V.A.2.a   Creating Records: PUT

> PUT is introduced here as the starting point for operations which are to be added in this and following chapters.
>
> PRINT can still be used in many operations that store data in files.
>
> Which option works best in a given situation will become clearer as special topics are introduced.

The PUT statement is used to create records. Each PUT transfers data from the computer's output buffer to the file. The file must be OPEN and assigned a channel number. The channel number is then used with the PUT statement.

PUT transfers data sequentially if no organizational technique is given, or if the organization is stated to be sequential. The default for a computer system is almost always sequential.

```
100 MAP (NAMES) NAME$ = 25%
200 OPEN 'IS200.DAT' FOR OUTPUT AS FILE #1      &
        , ORGANIZATION SEQUENTIAL               &
        , ACCESS WRITE                          &
        , MAP (NAMES)
        .
        .
        .
300 INPUT "Enter student's name ";NAME$
310 PUT #1
        .
        .
900 CLOSE #1
```

Here a new file is being opened for processing. Students' names are to be entered from a terminal and stored sequentially in the file. Each INPUT statement obtains a value from the terminal and stores it in the MAPped area called NAME$. If the student's name is less than 25 characters, it will be padded with blanks to the right until the storage area is filled. If it is longer than 25 characters it will be truncated to 25 characters.

Each PUT statement transfers the contents of the storage area NAMES to the file. While this operation is simple and straightforward, its implications for data management are many and varied. Study this example carefully.

V.A.2.b   Adding Records to File: APPEND

If data is to be added to an already existing sequential file, then it must be added logically at the end of the file. It must be APPENDed to the file. In sequential files, data records may not be added between existing records. The file must be opened for INPUT and ACCESS APPEND specified.

```
100 OPEN 'IS200.DAT' FOR INPUT AS FILE #1    &
        , ORGANIZATION SEQUENTIAL            &
        , ACCESS APPEND
```

To use PUT and APPEND together, the next-record pointer must indicate end-of-file. PUT does not point to a current record, and a simple OPEN for writing will not locate the end of a current file.

V.A.2.c   Locating Records: FIND

FIND is a special purpose BASIC instruction. It is used to advance the current-record pointer to a given record, without retrieving all the records in between. Suppose that one wanted to retrieve a record of a student, and that the records for each student were stored sequentially and alphabetically as in the professor's grade book: Abel = 1, Baker = 2, Charley = 3, etc.

```
100 OPEN 'IS200.DAT' FOR INPUT AS FILE #1    &
        , ORGANIZATION SEQUENTIAL            &
        , ACCESS READ
        .
        .
        .
200 INPUT "Enter student's number ";NUMB
300 FIND #1 FOR X = 1 TO NUMB
        .
        .
```

FIND is used here to bypass all the records between the beginning of the file and NUMB number of records. The current-record pointer is then left at the record NUMB for retrievel. FIND does not cause data to be moved. It simply changes the position of the current and next-record pointers.

FIND is a special verb which works faster than INPUT (or GET) because no data is moved. Both INPUT and GET work equally well for sequential reads and writes.

V.A.2.d   Retrieving Records: GET

The GET statement moves data from the file into the computer's internal memory. If FIND is used to position the current-record pointer, the GET statement retrieves the contents of the current record. When GET is used alone, each successive GET retrieves the *next* record.

```
100 MAP (NAMES) NAME$ = 25%
200 OPEN 'IS200.DAT' FOR INPUT AS FILE #1        &
            , ORGANIZATION SEQUENTIAL               &
            , ACCESS READ                           &
            , MAP NAMES
       .
       .
300 GET #1
310 PRINT NAME$
       .
       .
900 CLOSE #1
```

GET moves data from the file to the storage area NAMES, where it can be referenced by the variable NAME$.

Note how a small network is created within the BASIC program. In line 300, GET _#1 references the file on channel _#1, which is specified in line 200. The MAP NAMES, in statement 200, in turn references the variable string NAME$ in line 100. Line 310 then prints the contents of this variable.

> from GET #1 (line 300)
> to →MAP NAMES (line 200)
> to →NAME$ = 25% (line 100)
> to →PRINT NAME$ (line 310)

GET statements, when used with MAP, PUT, and FIND statements, offer a powerful tool for data and information processing. Sequential files may at times be cumbersome, but when used with proper thought and planning, they can often be more efficiently and more quickly processed than other file organizations.

V.A.2.e Searching Records: GET WHILE

In BASIC, WHILE is used to repeatedly modify a statement as long as a given logical expression or relation is *true*. When used with GET, WHILE causes records to be retrieved and examined until a field or fields contain the needed data. Often this relation is stated negatively, for example:

```
ln   GET WHILE relation-1 <> relation-2

300 GET WHILE "John Doe" <> NAME$
```

The above statement causes a search for the name "John Doe". As long as the NAME$ field does not contain the value "John Doe", a new record will be read and examined. When the NAME$ field does equal "John Doe" the search will be ended.

V.A.2.f Updating Records: UPDATE

Individual records can be UPDATEd, or changed, in a sequential file without accessing other records in the file. It is not necessary for the whole file to be searched and copied to a new file as individual records are changed.

The UPDATE statement permits individual pieces of data to be changed without the need to process the whole file. It must at the same time be used with consideration because once data is changed, it is changed (!) and previous values are gone. If a copy of the original data is needed, then a backup copy of the file must be created before the file is to be opened for processing.

GET is first used to copy the data from the record to the buffer. The contents of the buffer are changed, and UPDATE is used to *replace* the existing data in the file.

Suppose in the professor's student file a name has been incorrectly entered, JOMES for JONES. This error could be corrected as follows.

```
100 MAP (NAMES) NAME$ = 25%
200 OPEN 'IS200.DAT' FOR INPUT AS FILE #1     &
         , ORGANIZATION SEQUENTIAL             &
         , ACCESS MODIFY                       &
         , MAP NAMES
         .
         .
         .
300 INPUT "Student name to be changed ";OLD_NAME$
310 GET #1 WHILE OLD_NAME$ <>NAME$
320 INPUT "Enter new name ";NAME$
330 UPDATE #1
         .
         .
900 CLOSE #1
```

Note that the ACCESS is MODIFY, and that once NAME$ is entered in line 330, the MAP variable has a new value from the one obtained through the GET statement.

from GET #1 (line 310) when OLD_NAME$ (line 300)
                                    = NAME$ (line 310)

   to ⎣→INPUT NAME$ (line 320)

     to ⎣→UPDATE #1 (line 330)

GET copies the record from the file to the buffer. The INPUT statement then receives a new value from the terminal, and it is this new value that will then be stored by the UPDATE command.

Another GET would copy the next record, or the file may again be searched sequentially using GET WHILE. Notice that the process does not go directly to the record and copy the data. Each of the previous records is copied and examined before the needed data is identified. On smaller files, or files where data most likely to be updated has been sorted or located at the beginning of the file, the operations described above cause few problems. Sequential search and update operations can, however, become expensive and inefficient if used without forethought and planning before the file is ever created. And again, take heed—no backup file is created with the UPDATE command.

V.A.2.g   File Truncation: SCRATCH

In current versions of BASIC, individual records cannot be deleted from a file.

In many data and information systems, this limitation causes few problems. In business systems, for example, records are not deleted; they are "flagged" as containing inactive data. This simply means that somewhere in the record a character—or other indicator—is written, which indicates to the program and its users that the data in the record is not considered active. This indicator can, of course, be changed back, in the same manner that one might close and reopen a business account. Later, such records may be copied to a "history" file, and a new file created without these records.

A file can be truncated by having records deleted from a certain point to the end of the file. New records can then be added from this point. The ACCESS method used in this instance is SCRATCH.

```
100 OPEN "IS200.DAT" FOR INPUT AS FILE #1      &
        , ORGANIZATION SEQUENTIAL              &
        , ACCESS SCRATCH

     .
     .

200 INPUT "Enter number of records to save ";NUMB_RECS
210 FIND #1 FOR X = 1 TO (NUMB_RECS +1)
220 SCRATCH #1

     .
     .
```

Since SCRATCH deletes records from the current-record pointer to the end of the file, it is necessary in the above example to add 1 to NUMB___RECS to be saved so that the current-record pointer will set at the first record to be deleted.

V.B MAGNETIC TAPE PROCESSING

This section may appear to contain a little more detail than usual for sequential files. Large computer systems have in-house programs available for reading, writing, and copying magnetic tapes. Some even make enough disk storage available so that entire files can be copied before processing. When everything runs as anticipated for the majority of tape users, then tape operations can be completed with a minimum of help.

It is when something a little different is needed that the user comes to the data professional for help. "I need to reformat over

100,000 lines so that the center part of each line is removed; and those lines that end with an asterisk should have their line number increased by 10,000. Can you help me?" Such requests are *not* uncommon. There are no vendor-supplied routines to handle them. It is up to an individual to write a program to reformat the data, using tape for input and output.

The following presents an introduction to the various aspects of magnetic tape processing. The different requests for problem solutions will occur in real life quickly enough.

NOTE: Before a magnetic tape can be processed by BASIC, a tape drive must first be allocated, and a magnetic tape mounted on the drive.

A device name must also be established for the drive. Instructions for this step should be obtained from the computer center staff.

The device name used here is:

MT1:

Perhaps the best examples of sequential files are files stored on magnetic tape. This is, of course, inherent in the nature of the device. Just as music is stored sequentially on a cassette recording, data is stored from some starting point on the tape until there is no more data to be stored. When data is retrieved from the tape, it is retrieved in the order in which it was stored.

But in contrast to the use of music cassettes where the listener can run the tape backward and forward until he or she hears the beginning of a particular piece of music, the computer cannot hear its data. It can only work forward from some established beginning point.

In some aspects, magnetic tape can prove limiting. It would be easy to become impatient at a bank window, waiting for information on an account while someone loaded a tape and invoked a special program to search for our piece of data. Magnetic tapes are not really suited for this type of an operation. Some operations are best left to disk systems.

Yet there remain a great many operations for which magnetic tapes are ideally suited. One of these operations is "batch" processing, in which transaction files are "posted", or run, against master files. Blocks of data can be read and processed sequentially, without the need for the searching routines common with disk directories. Batch systems easily generate backup copies of master files, should a particular job abort and need restarting.

Magnetic tapes are also an excellent off-line storage media. Since backup procedures are designed to provide another copy of the data, should the system or a process fail (and they sometimes do), the manner of storing and retrieving the data need only be simple, quick, and straightforward—i.e., sequential. Start at some point and read to a storage medium until finished. Retrieval works in the opposite direction, putting everything back where it was.

In addition, magnetic tapes are inexpensive and durable; and when compared with the cost of disk packs, they are extremely inexpensive. Most off-line storage of large volumes of data is, therefore, on magnetic tape. In the early days of data processing, files were basically sequential, and this is, of course, no longer the case; but sequential files have not become old-fashioned or restricted to small files on disk. They are found as basic components of a great many computer operations.

V.B.1   Device Names: OPEN

Usually computer systems are programmed to find data on a disk pack, unless otherwise specified. A simple OPEN for a file defaults to a search for the file on disk. If the system is to look for the file elsewhere, it must be prompted to do so. When magnetic tape is to hold the data, a device name is added before the file name.

```
OPEN 'device:filename.ext' FOR ......

ln OPEN 'MT1:IS200.DAT' FOR OUTPUT AS FILE #1 &
        [,ORGANIZATION SEQUENTIAL [FIXED,VARIABLE]]  &
        [,ACCESS WRITE]                              &
        [,BLOCKSIZE 10 ]                             &
        [,RECORDSIZE 80]                             &
        [,NOREWIND]

[ ] = options
```

Here the device name "MT1:" precedes the file name. This causes the magnetic tape on device "MT1:" to become the storage medium. Each time data is to be stored, it will be written on the tape. By explicitly specifying the device in the OPEN statement, the system default is said to be "overridden".

V.B.2   Positioning the Tape: NOREWIND

Data is written sequentially on a magnetic tape from a predeter-mined starting point until there is no more data. The tape drive automatically locates the beginning-of-tape (BOT) point, and it will not permit data to be written beyond the physical end-of-tape (EOT). As characters are written a block at a time to a magnetic tape, the drive advances the tape, putting inner-block-gaps (IBG) between the blocks. This gap is about 3/4 inch in length and is the space needed to start and stop the tape. When a file is closed, an end-of-file (EOF) mark and a logical-end-of-tape (LOT) mark are written on the tape.

B		E L		E
O	blocks/gaps	O O		O
T		F T		T

When a second file is written to the tape, the process is repeated from the previous logical-end-of-tape mark.

B		E		E L		E
O	characters/gaps	O	characters/gaps	O O		O
T		F		F T		T

      File 1   File 2

In order for this to happen without mishap, it is necessary to advance the tape to the end-of-file mark before beginning to write a new file. Failure to do so will most likely mean loss of data.

Suppose someone forgot to advance the tape before writing a third file on the tape above; the results would look like this if the third file were larger than the first.

B		E L		E L		E
O	characters/gaps	O O	cters/gaps	O O		O
T		F T		F T		T

      File 3   File 2

Since the tape is always read and advanced sequentially, all data after the first LOT would, in effect, be deleted.

> As data is being written to a tape, any previous data and tape marks are also being written over. They are gone forever, and new data have taken their place. It is, therefore, always wise to consider carefully how a particular tape is to be used before opening a tape file for processing.

V.B.2.a   OPEN FOR OUTPUT

The default positioning statement for a magnetic tape is REWIND. This means that when a file is opened for output, the tape will be positioned at the BOT mark.

When NOREWIND is specified, and the tape is opened for output, the tape will be advanced to the LOT mark before data is written.

```
100 OPEN "MT1:IS200.DAT" FOR OUTPUT AS FILE #2     &
        , ORGANIZATION SEQUENTIAL                  &
        , NOREWIND
```

If there already is data on the tape and it is *not* to be overwritten, then NOREWIND must be specified in the OPEN statement.

V.B.2.b   OPEN FOR INPUT

Here the chance for error is not so great as when writing to a tape. When a particular file is requested, the tape will be positioned at the BOT mark (rewound if necessary) and a search begun for the file. If the file is found, the tape will be positioned at the beginning of the file ready for processing. If the file is not found, an error message will be generated.

NOREWIND has virtually the same effect, except that when NOREWIND is specified, the search is begun from the current tape position, beginning or otherwise. When a LOT mark is found, the tape is rewound and the search renewed. If the file is then not found, an error message is generated.

V.B.2.c   Data Handling: RECORDSIZE/BLOCKSIZE

RECORDSIZE sets the number of characters that will logically make up a record.

```
100 OPEN "MT1: IS200. DAT" FOR OUTPUT AS FILE #2     &
        , ORGANIZATION SEQUENTIAL                   &
        , RECORDSIZE 80%                            &
        , NOREWIND
```

In this case, a block of data will contain 80 characters, or one record. Each write to the tape will cause a pause in operation and a transfer of 80 characters to the tape, followed by an inner-block gap.

```
+------------------------------------- · · · ------+
| B            I            I                      |
| O   80chrs   B   80chrs   B   · · ·              |
| T            G            G                      |
+------------------------------------- · · · ------+
```

This is, of course, not the most effecient manner of storing records on magnetic tape. Each time 80 characters are written to the tape, a shift in operations must occur. This shift in turn slows processing. The inner-block gaps also occur after each record.

Much of this loss of processing time and tape space can be prevented by specifying a BLOCKSIZE in the OPEN statement. BLOCKSIZE specifies a multiple of the characters indicated in the RECORDSIZE option.

```
100 OPEN "MT1: IS200. DAT" FOR OUTPUT AS FILE #2 &
        , ORGANIZATION SEQUENTIAL                &
        , RECORDSIZE 80%                         &
        , BLOCKSIZE 10%
```

This statement forms a buffer of 800 (80 x 10) characters. When the buffer is full, then all 800 characters will be written at the same time. Such blocking greatly decreases processing time, while eliminating unnecessary inner-block gaps.

V.B.3   Reading and Writing Tapes: PUT/GET

As described above, PUT and GET are used to read and write sequential tape files. PUT moves one logical record to the output buffer; and when the buffer is full, it will be written to tape. GET works in the opposite direction, from tape to buffer to user area.

```
200 GET #1, A$
210 PRINT A$
```

```
200 INPUT A$
210 PUT #1, A$ = 80%
```

V.B.4   Closing the File: CLOSE

CLOSE closes the channel to the tape file. It works the same as for any file, whether on tape or disk.

`ln CLOSE #n`

When the CLOSE statement is executed with tape files, an end-of-file and a logical-end-of-tape mark are written to the tape.

> After the BASIC has terminated, the drive must still be rewound, the tape dismounted, and the drive deallocated (REWIND, DISMOUNT, DEALLOCATE). Refer to the system manual for formatting and usage rules.

V.C   BATCH PROCESSING

Traditional data processing has been and continues to be BATCH processing. BATCH implies that transactions or file updates are saved until there are enough to justify processing. For some time this has meant that a BATCH of computer cards was carefully checked and corrected until all of the data were ready for processing. Today, the same data is often stored on disk or diskette, and then edited interactively. The result is a transaction file of carefully prepared and edited data, ready for processing in a single operation.

Transaction files are "run against" master files. Whereas transaction files are usually created anew for each processing, master files tend to be fairly stable over a period of time. In a payroll system, the master file would contain data about the employee—i.e., employee number, name, address, pay grades, etc.; and a new transaction file would be created for each time period, containing the employee number and the hours worked. The latter file would then be carefully edited to ensure accuracy of its data, sorted in the same order as the master file, and processed sequentially to update the master file.

Not all data systems work exactly in this manner, but transaction and master files form the core of a great many data processing operations. It is also not necessary that the processing be done sequentially; but when larger sets of data are to be updated and the number of updates is not small, sequential file updates can provide efficient and economical use of system resources. The usual process contains four basic steps:

1. Prepare and edit transactions
2. Sort and run transactions against master records
3. Create a backup copy of the master file
4. Generate reports

The first step is extremely important. It might even be the most important. All of the steps are, of course, important to a data system; but if incorrect data can be kept out of a data system through carefully designed controls and editing procedures, then the chances of a data system's having a long and successful life are greatly enhanced. It is not only exasperating to be constantly correcting incorrect information on reports, but also extremely expensive. Once a master file gets incorrect data in it, its value is so severely diminished as to render it almost useless. Every precaution must, therefore, be taken to ensure that this first step is always completed as accurately as possible.

The second step, once written and tested, seldom creates problems. Care should be taken when designing the program to include error checking routines. The program should catch attempts to update nonexistent accounts, or to add already existing accounts. Master file records are also never simply deleted; rather they are marked as inactive by adding an indicator, or "flag", somewhere in the record signifying that the data in the record is considered to be inactive. These records can later be identified and copied to a history file before being removed from the master file.

Once the transaction file is sorted by key in the same order as the master file, processing begins by matching keys and updating records until the transaction file is completely processed. All anomalies are printed, or "logged", for appropriate action.

In the diagram at the top of page 105, a backup file is automatically created because the current master becomes "old" once the new master is created. It can be saved along with the transaction file in case the new master is for some reason lost or destroyed.

The update program would be similar to the program flow shown in the second diagram on page 105 if both files contain keys sorted in ascending order.

Note in the matching process that whenever a transaction key is larger than the key in the master file (T>M), then a transaction exists for a nonexistent account and an error situation occurs.

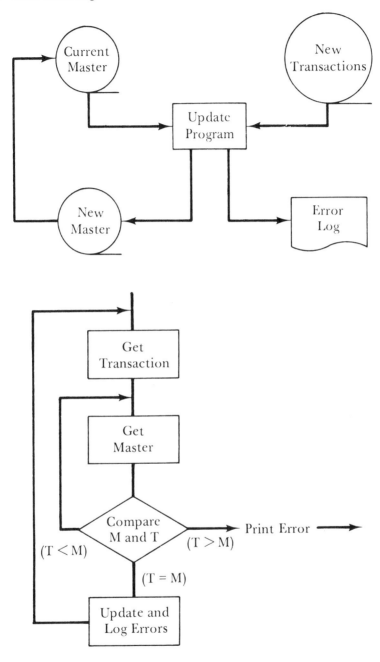

Sequential batch processing as it is briefly described here does not give the user immediate control of his or her data in the master file. Reports have to wait until a batch is created and a run against the master file initiated. There is nothing immediate about a batch system.

Yet the advantages of such a system are often overlooked. When there are a great many transactions and when they can be batched, processing is usually fast and economical. But even this consideration is not the most important consideration. Sometimes the most economical data processing system is not the best for a given situation.

The real advantage to batch processing is that it runs in a carefully controlled environment. Interactive updating of master files must be done with great care even in a small, well controlled system; but in a large system, it is almost always unacceptable, except in very special circumstances. Batch updating of master files is in itself no guarantee of data accuracy, but it does offer better planning, use, and control of resources, including data entry.

The system described above also provides automatic backup and restarting points should something fail to function as expected—and this is an important consideration. In a data system, one cannot wait for something to go wrong before taking action. Good data systems contain predetermined restarting points. If something should then go amiss, proper action can be undertaken promptly and with the assurance that the system will be restarted accurately and without loss of data.

As stated above, batch systems are not limited to sequential files, or for that matter to sequential files stored on magnetic tape. Most large data systems, however, contain batch operations, and some find it useful to store their data on magnetic tape. Neither batch systems nor magnetic tape have been relegated to the halls of information history, and they should always be considered as possible options when analyzing and designing data and information systems.

V.D SAMPLE PROGRAM

Request: A magnetic tape contains an alphabetized concordance of a medieval German epic of over 100,000 records. It is sorted alphabetically by the word form, beginning in column 1.

Word form (1–20)	Line number (21–25)	Text (26–80)
an	6624	Tristan den schilt an sich gewan,

The program is to obtain a first letter from which to begin and a final letter with which to end. It is then to transfer all records (and all intervening records) beginning with these letters to a second tape. A subset of the first tape is, therefore, to be created.

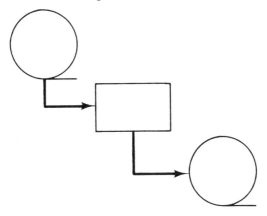

Tape 1 ———→ Program ———→ Tape 2

Record layout:

L$	1	A	First letter of record
REST$	79	A	Rest of record

Process:

1– OPEN two tape files
2– INPUT beginning and ending letters
3– GET input tape until L$ = BEG$
4– GET and PUT records until L$ > LAST$
5– CLOSE files

```
10 ON ERROR GOTO 700
20                                                          REM
100 MAP (REC)    L$ = 1%, REST$ = 79%
110                                                         REM
200 OPEN "TAPE.CON" FOR INPUT AS FILE #1                    &
         , ORGANIZATION SEQUENTIAL VARIABLE                 &
         , ACCESS READ                                      &
         , MAP REC
250                                                         REM
```

```
252 REM ******************************************
254 REM *                                        *
256 REM * Obtain starting and ending points      *
258 REM *                                        *
259 REM ******************************************
260                                                        REM
300 PRINT \ INPUT "Enter beginning letter "; BEG$
310 PRINT \ INPUT "Enter ending letter    "; LAST$
320                                                        REM
350 REM ******************************************
352 REM *                                        *
354 REM * Use letters to create file name        *
356 REM * Open output file                       *
358 REM *                                        *
360 REM ******************************************
362                                                        REM
370 FIL$ = BEG$ + LAST$ + ".DAT"
375                                                        REM
380 OPEN FIL$ FOR OUTPUT AS FILE #2                        &
          , ORGANIZATION SEQUENTIAL VARIABLE               &
          , ACCESS WRITE                                   &
          , MAP REC
390                                                        REM
400 REM ******************************************
402 REM *                                        *
404 REM * Search for beginning point             *
406 REM *                                        *
408 REM ******************************************
410                                                        REM
500 GET #1
510    IF L$ = BEG$ THEN 600
520 GOTO 500
530                                                        REM
```

```
550 REM *******************************************
552 REM *                                         *
554 REM * Transfer records until end point        *
556 REM *                                         *
558 REM *******************************************
560                                                   REM
600 PRINT PRINT "At letter ";L$;" ";REST$ GOTO 620
610 GET #1
615    IF L$ = LAST$ THEN 630
620    IF L$ > LAST$ THEN 800
630 PUT #2
640 GOTO 610
650                                                   REM
700 RESUME 710
710 PRINT ERL;"   ";ERT$(ERR);"   ";ERR
720                                                   REM
800 PRINT \ PRINT "Stopped at ";L$;" ";REST$
810 CLOSE #1 \ CLOSE #2
820 END
```

V.E REVIEW QUESTIONS

1. How are sequential files created logically and physically? Explain the processes for adding and deleting records for a sequential file.

2. What is meant by the term *batch processing*? Is it still used today? Why?

3. Explain how magnetic tapes are used to store data. What are blocks and interrecord gaps? What roles do they play when tapes are used?

4. How big is a buffer for 80 character records with a blocksize of 100? Can your computer handle this blocksize?

5. Given some of the normal uses for tapes described in this chapter, what do you think would be the minimum number of tape drives needed for a data processing operation? Why?

6. When more than one file is to be used in a program, how does the program know which file is which? What are computer channels? How are they used?

7. What is the difference between the FIND and GET statements? Which is faster?

8. How is data updated in sequential files? Because this process can be slow, how might a job be set to minimize processing?

V.F. EXERCISES

1. Design a record layout and write a program to create a sequential file using data similar to the example. Each record should be 80 characters in length.

Joe Spizak   1602 Kingston Dr.   Greentown, NY 10013

2. Design a system flowchart and write a program that will search the above file sequentially, displaying each record on a terminal and asking if the record is to be deleted. If the answer is Yes, then delete the record (after checking to be sure). If the answer is not Yes, then write the record to a second file.

3. Check the manuals and handouts in your computer center for explanations on using magnetic tapes. Using a scratch tape provided by your instructor, rewrite and test exercise 1.

4. Set up a project to maintain a checkbook. Include all documentaion. At the end of each month, all returned checks are to be sorted manually and then entered through a terminal into a sequential file. This file is then to be posted against the check master file. A statement for the month is also to be printed. Be sure to handle all possibilities. What happens if a check is not returned? Or if one comes in that is three months old? How will deposits be handled?

a. State the problem in your own words.

b. Be sure you can do each step manually. Use test data to arrive at correct results; and be sure the test data includes all situations and problems.

c. Design the system flowchart and record layouts.

d. Design a flowchart, or top-down diagram to illustrate the data flow.

e. Manually walk the test data through the solution charted in **d**. Be sure all results are correct.

Now write and test the program.

VI
Relative Files

VI.A PHYSICAL ORGANIZATION

When processing data, it is often useful to be able to access data stored in individual records without examining the contents of other records. One can only imagine the time it would take at a bank teller's window if all records stored before the current customer's had to be searched before a transaction could be completed. It would make no difference whether the search was done manually through metal file drawers or by a computer through sequential files on magnetic tape. The time consumed would not be acceptable in a modern business. In order to avoid unnecessary search and retrieval delays in manual systems, an organized system is developed whereby one can go directly to a file drawer and then alphabetically or numerically quickly find the needed data.

On computer systems, similar access methods have also been developed. They are generally called RANDOM, or DIRECT access systems, and use disks or diskettes as data storage devices. DIRECT usually refers to the storage device itself, and RANDOM the manner of accessing the data. On some microcomputer systems, however, relative files are called direct access files.

Random Access permits individual records to be accessed without examining the contents of other records. The data is organized by the system and stored on disk(ette)s. One might imagine a disk system as being similar to a record player, where the arm can be positioned at any point on the record at any time. On disk systems, a read–write head can be positioned directly before the needed data. Provided the system "knows" where the data is located, there is no need for a sequential search. And like a record, where the music can be played from beginning to end, data stored on disk can still be processed sequentially, from beginning to end.

Magnetic tapes are usually limited to storing data organized sequentially. Disk systems also process sequential files, but two additonal organizations can be used with disk systems: *Relative* and *Indexed*. Both of these methods store data so that individual records can be stored and retrieved without accessing the contents of other records. This chapter presents relative files; the next indexed files.

VI.A.1   Relative vs. Sequential Files

Sequential files are processed from beginning to end. Relative files may be processed from beginning to end; but in addition, each record can be acessed directly by value of a key. As it is being stored, each record is assigned a logical position within the file. The record's key becomes its position *relative* to the beginning of the file.

"Relative" implies, then, that each record is somehow logically positioned in relation to every other record in the file. The first record in the file is assigned the logical position of #1, the next record the logical position of #2, the third the logical position of #3, etc. Thus, each record after the first is *relative* in *logical position* to the first record. The 43rd record would be number 43 in a series.

One might consider a relative file to be a series of cells, numbered sequentially, 1, 2, 3, 4, 5, etc.

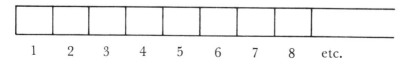

Each record is assigned a number and its contents placed in the corresponding cell. If we have 12 salespersons, we might assign each an individual number from 1 to 12. The data for each salesperson would be stored in the cell assigned to their particular number. The assigned number would be the *key*: a key to the relative location of the record.

Records are added by moving data to empty cells. Records are deleted by moving spaces, nulls, or another record to the cell where the current record is stored. Records are updated by copying the contents of a record into the CPU, changing values of a field or fields, and then rewriting the new contents back to the same cell.

As far as the programmer is concerned, this is a logical process. The actual physical location of the record on the disk is left to the operating system. Unless one is dealing with a much older disk system, it is not usually necessary to know exactly how this process takes place.

The problem with older systems was that is was necessary to specify in advance the number of cells to be included in a file before a file could be created. If the actual number of records varied greatly over a period of time, the empty cells represented wasted space. Modern disk systems are designed to store data as efficiently as possible. They have ways of minimizing wasted space, and as a result, the application programmer can select the best method for logically handling data without becoming overly concerned with physical considerations.

The real advantage of relative files over sequential files is the ability to access an individual record both sequentially and randomly. Records can be updated and deleted without disturbing other records; and records can be inserted into empty cells at any time.

Note carefully, however, that a new dimension is being added here! Where sequential files easily led to backup files in case of human, machine, or environmental problems, now it is a simple matter to quickly delete, erase, destroy, incorrectly update, etc., a record's contents and lose important data. Extra care must now be taken so that data is protected. In most data systems, data must never be easily and simply deleted from the system! Always ask "What happens if ....?" and design the system accordingly—when necessary with sequential backups.

VI.A.2   Keys

For each record in a relative file, there exists a key which tells the location of the record, relative to the beginning of the file. This key may, or may not, be included as a field within the record. When it is not within the record, then a list of used and unused keys must be kept somewhere or one would forget which key referenced which record. Keys are, therefore, usually also found within a field in each record. A listing of the file also lists the keys.

No matter where they are kept, *keys for each record must be unique.* An individual key must reference an individual cell; for example, two salespersons with the same key would result in confusion and probable loss of data. Care must, therefore, be taken in assigning and using keys.

VI.A.2.a Uncoded Keys

Uncoded keys have a one-to-one relationship between the record's key and its position within the file. Key #1 indicates cell #1. An example might be a teacher's grade book, where the students are numbered down the page from one to however many students are in the course. The 3rd student down the page is #3, the 5th is #5, etc. To access a record, find the student's number in the grade book, enter the number when prompted by the program, and the record will be available for processing. This is the simplest method and the one used in the program examples in this chapter.

VI.A.2.b Coded/Hashed Keys

It is not always possible to use uncoded keys. There may simply be no correspondence between the relative position of the record and the key used to store the record. Some values within data records are natural keys, such as inventory numbers, part numbers, social security numbers, license plate numbers, etc. To create uncoded keys in such instances might not be worth the effort.

Suppose that we have a maximum of 25 salespersons in our staff, but their number of reference within the organization is the same as their district—three-digit numbers between 001 and 999. With uncoded keys, this could mean in an older system a total of 999 cells to store only 25 records. On modern disk systems this would not be a problem because the disk system would not actually allocate a cell until it was needed, and its physical location would not necessarily be next to another cell in the same file.

But on older disk systems, where cells must be allocated before the file can be opened, and where cells are considered to be physically contiguous, there would be a potential for a lot of wasted space. On such systems, an arithmetic formula is used to calculate the relative location of the cells to be used. Some rather elaborate formulas have been developed to create useful keys. The generic term used for this process is *Hash Coding*. It indicates a mathematical translation of the actual key to a relative key.

One hashing method, which can be used as an example, is termed the *division/remainder* method. A prime number closest to the needed number of cells is chosen. Prime numbers—i.e., numbers which can be divided only by 1 and by themselves—are used because they give better results. The actual key is divided by the prime number, and the *remainder* becomes the relative position of the cell.

For example, if 23 is the prime number chosen for the 25 needed cells, and our salesperson is assigned district 528, then:

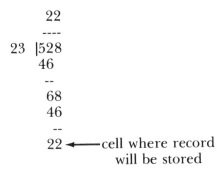

```
           22
          ----
    23  |528
           46
           --
           68
           46
           --
           22  ←——cell where record
                   will be stored
```

In an ideal situation, one need only generate a few arithmetic instructions and the relative location of the cell is known. This can be followed by a simple disk read and the contents of the record become available.

Such situations are, of course, not always ideal. Suppose we have two districts, numbered 806 and 507 respectively, and our prime number is still 23.

```
        35                        22
       ----                      ----
 23  |806                  23  |507
       69                         46
       --                         --
      116                         47
      115                         46
      ---                         --
        1  ←——collision——→         1
```

When the hashing algorithm generates the same cell for two different keys, a collision results which could mean the loss of data.

In these cases, it is necessary to further refine the system by using overflow areas whenever a cell already contains data.

Note also that if the file were to be processed sequentially from beginning to end, the records would not necessarily be in order by logical key. They would be in the order of the cell in which they were stored. It would be necessary to process the file from a list of pre-sorted keys to get a true sequential listing of the contents of the file.

There are some quite sophisticated hashing schemes available. The generation of such schemes has become a science in itself. Nonetheless, it is best whenever possible to use a more modern disk system or a logical assignment of keys so that hashing is unnecessary. An example might be storing and retrieving tables and arrays.

Even if the disk system demands physically contiguous cells, relative files with easy to recognize and manage keys present a very quick and efficient means of storing and retrieving data.

VI.B PROCESSING RELATIVE FILES

VI.B.1 Definition: OPEN

Since relative files are considered logically to consist of a series of cells stored on disk, it is necessary to define the size of each cell.

If a MAP statement is used, then the buffer is considered to be *static*. Each cell will contain the same number of bytes.

```
100 MAP (RELSRC)    SOC__SEC$     =    9%  &
                    , NAME$       =   20%  &
                    , ADDRESS$    =   20%  &
                    , CITY__STATE$ =  20%  &
                    , ZIP%
200 OPEN 'RELFLE.DAT' FOR OUTPUT AS FILE #1   &
         , ORGANIZATION RELATIVE              &
         , MAP RELREC
```

The OPEN statement establishes the name (RELFLE.DAT) for the file, ORGANIZATION is defined as RELATIVE, and the MAP statement contains the size of each cell. Since each cell will contain the same amount of data, they are considered to be static. Data values are automatically stored in the MAPped variables for storing and retrieving.

It is also possible to give a maximum size for the record buffer using the RECORDSIZE option in the OPEN statement.

```
200 OPEN 'RELFLE.DAT' FOR OUTPUT AS FILE #1   &
          , ORGANIZATION RELATIVE              &
          , RECORDSIZE = 80%
```

In this case, data values are assigned to variables; the variables are MOVED TO the assigned channel and then written. This process is considered to be *dynamic*.

If the file already exists, it is OPENed for INPUT regardless of the operation to be performed. The OPEN statement must also contain an ORGANIZATION option to instruct the system on how to process the records. The buffers will also be assigned for static or dynamic processing.

```
200 OPEN 'RELFLE.DAT' FOR INPUT AS FILE #1   &
          , ORGANIZATION RELATIVE             &
          , RECORDSIZE = 80%
```

VI.B.2 Writing Records: PUT

When records are written to relative files, they may be written either sequentially or randomly. The PUT statement is used to move data from the buffer to a cell. If the cell number is not given, then the next-record pointer indicates which logical cell is to be used.

(A) Static (MAP)

(1) ln PUT #n   400 PUT #1
(2) ln PUT #n, RECORD # 400 PUT #1, RECORD 20

(B) Dynamic (RECORDSIZE)

(1) ln MOVE TO #n   350 MOVE TO #1, CAT$ = 10%, DOG$ = 10%
        ln PUT #n   400 PUT #1
(2) ln MOVE TO #n   350 MOVE TO #1, CAT$ = 10%, DOG$ = 10%
        ln PUT #n, RECORD n 400 PUT #1, RECORD 20

In example A1 above, data stored in the MAPped areas will be PUT sequentially to the next cell. In A2, the data will be PUT randomly to cell number 20. With dynamic allocation, the MOVE TO statement moves data values to the buffer/channel, and the PUT statement then writes the contents of the buffer to disk.

The following program is an example of static buffering. The PART_NO% in line 520, which is supposed to be a number between 1 and 25 (0 = END), is also used in line 550 as the location of the record cell.

```
200 MAP (RELREC)  PART_NO%                    &
                , NAME$         = 20%         &
                , COST
300 OPEN 'RELREC. DAT' FOR OUTPUT AS FILE #1  &
          , ORGANIZATION RELATIVE             &
          , MAP RELREC
400 ON ERROR GOTO 600
500                                                      REM
510 FOR I = 1 TO 25
520     INPUT "PART NUMBER (0, 1-25) ==> "; PART_NO%
525        IF PART_NO% > 25 THEN PRINT "Incorrect number" \ &
                              GOTO 520
530        IF PART_NO% = 0 THEN 710
540     INPUT "PART DESCRIPTION [20] ==> "; NAME$
545     INPUT "COST [NO $ SIGN]      ==> "; COST
550     PUT #1, RECORD PART_NO%
560        IF I = 24 THEN PRINT "*** last entry ***"
570 NEXT I
580 GOTO 710
600                                                      REM
610 IF (ERR = 153%) THEN RESUME 630          &
       ELSE ON ERROR GOTO 0
620                                                      REM
630 PRINT \ PRINT "PART NUMBER "; PART_NO%; " ALREADY EXISTS"
640 GOTO 520
700                                                      REM
710 PRINT "RELREC. DAT = "; I; " RECORDS"
720 CLOSE #1
730 END
```

Note the use of ON ERROR in line 400 to check for duplicate part numbers. Also remember that once OPENed, files must be CLOSEd (line 720).

VI.B.3 Locating Records: FIND

FIND locates data, but does not move it from the disk. When processing relative files sequentially, FIND skips empty cells and moves the current-record pointer to the next cell containing data.

ln FIND #n

400 FIND #1

When a record cell is specified, then FIND sets the record-pointer to the specified cell.

ln FIND #n, RECORD #

400 FIND #1, RECORD 20

Should the record not exist, ERR = 155% (RECORD NOT FOUND) is returned.

VI.B.4   Retrieving Records: GET

GET moves a copy of the data stored in a relative cell into the record buffer. It can be used either with or without the FIND statement, and either sequentially or randomly.

ln GET #n

    (A) Sequentially

        (1) 400 GET #1
        (2) 350 FIND #1
             400 GET #1

    (B) Randomly

        (1) 400 GET #1, RECORD 20
        (2) 350 FIND #1, RECORD 20
             400 GET #1

A GET used alone moves the record pointers. When used with FIND, GET does not move record pointers; they are moved by the FIND statement.

Note the differences between A and B. Example A1 and, in some cases, A2 might attempt to retrieve data from logically empty cells, including end-of-files (ERR = 11). The program must account for this possibility using the ON ERROR routines. "RECORD NOT FOUND" (ERR = 155) is returned, should the record not exist. This error message is the same for both the FIND and the GET statements.

After a random GET, the file may be processed sequentially, beginning with the next record.

```
300 GET #1, RECORD 21
     .
     .
     .
400 GET #1
```

When used with MAP statements, GET works the same as with the PUT statement. Note the sample program at the end of the chapter.

VI.B.5   Modifying Records: UPDATE

UPDATE is used to change the contents of a relative record. The process is as follows. Locate the record (FIND), copy it into memory (GET), modify it as needed, and then rewrite the whole record back to disk (UPDATE). UPDATE will not work unless a successful GET has been performed.

This process should be used with care. Once data is modified and rewritten to disk, the original data is gone! It is usually wise to keep backups for files that are modified from a terminal.

```
ln UPDATE #n

300 GET #1
     .
     INPUT . . . . . . all changes
     .
400 UPDATE #1
```

Once the data is in the buffer through a GET, any field or fields may be changed. UPDATE then uses this new data to *overwrite* the contents of the location where the original data was stored.

ACCESS MODIFY should also be specified in the OPEN statement when using UPDATE commands.

```
200 OPEN 'RELFLE.DAT' FOR INPUT AS FILE #1 &
         , ORGANIZATION RELATIVE            &
         , ACCESS MODIFY
```

VI.B.6   Deleting Records: DELETE

Again, caution is in order. Like UPDATE, DELETE removes data from a file! Failure to handle data with care can result not only in loss of valuable data, but also in hours of work reconstructing a file's contents.

As with UPDATE, DELETE uses FIND and/or GET to make sure the record exists. *Then the contents of the record should be checked to make sure it is the correct record.* Example A shows how data can be quickly deleted. Example B uses more caution.

```
ln DELETE #N
```

(A) 300 FIND #1, RECORD 20
     400 DELETE #1

(B) 300 GET #1, RECORD 20
     310 MOVE FROM #1 ... data ...
     320 PRINT ... data ...
     330 INPUT "DELETE (Y/N) ? ==> "; ANS$
     400 IF ANS$ = "Y" THEN DELETE #1

VI.B.7   Sample Program

The following rather limited program maintains a small inventory file. Part numbers are between 1 and 25, with the part number also being the same as the relative key for the record.

PART_NO%	2	N	Values: 1-25
NAME$	20	A	Part descript.
COST	6	N	999.99

```
100 MAP (RELREC)    PART_NO%              &
                    , NAME$      = 20%  &
                    , COST
150                                              REM
200 OPEN 'RELFLE.DAT' FOR INPUT AS FILE #1    &
             , ORGANIZATION RELATIVE           &
             , ACCESS MODIFY                   &
             , MAP RELREC
300                                              REM
400 ON ERROR GOTO 1100
500                                              REM
```

```
501 REM ******************************************
502 REM *                                        *
503 REM * Obtain part number (= relative key)    *
504 REM *                                        *
506 REM ******************************************
507                                                          REM
510 PRINT "           RELATIVE FILE UPDATE"
520 PRINT \ INPUT "PART NUMBER (0, 1-25) = = > "; PART_NO%
530          IF PART_NO% > 25 THEN PRINT "Incorrect number" \ &
                                    GOTO 520
540          IF PART_NO% = 0 THEN 1410
550 FIND #1, PART_NO%
600 REM ******************************************
601 REM *                                        *
602 REM *    Selection MENU                      *
603 REM *                                        *
604 REM ******************************************
605                                                          REM
610 PRINT \ PRINT "1 - EXAMINE"
620         PRINT "2 - UPDATE"
625         PRINT "3 - ADD"
630         INPUT "4 - DELETE        = = > "; NUMB%
640 ON NUMB% GOTO 700, 800, 1000, 900
650                                                          REM
652 REM ******************************************
654 REM *                                        *
656 REM *  700 = Display (examine) contents      *
658 REM *                                        *
660 REM ******************************************
662                                                          REM
700 GET #1 \ PRINT PART_NO%, NAME$, COST
710 GOTO 520
750                                                          REM
752 REM ******************************************
754 REM *                                        *
756 REM *  800 = Update NAME and COST            *
758 REM *                                        *
760 REM ******************************************
770                                                          REM
800 GET #1 \ PRINT "CURRENT DESCRIPTION  = = > "; NAME$, COST
820          INPUT "CHANGED NAME         = = > ";  NAME$
830          INPUT "CHANGED COST         = = > ";  COST
840 UPDATE #1 \ GOT 520
900                                                          REM
850                                                          REM
```

```
852 REM ****************************************
854 REM *                                     *
856 REM *  900 = Delete a record              *
858 REM *                                     *
860 REM ****************************************
862                                                          REM
900 PRINT \ PRINT "Do you want to delete part number ";    &
                                     PART_NO; "?"
920          INPUT " (Y/N)  = = > "; ANS$
930          IF ANS$ = "Y" THEN 940 ELSE 520
940 DELETE #1 \ GOTO 520
950                                                          REM
952 REM ****************************************
954 REM *                                     *
956 REM *  1000 = add a new record            *
958 REM *                                     *
960 REM ****************************************
962                                                          REM
1040                                                         REM
1050                                                         REM
1000 PRINT \ INPUT "INPUT PART NAME    = = > "; NAME$
1020          INPUT "ENTER COST (no $ sign) > "; COST
1030 PUT #1, RECORD PART_NO% GOTO 520
1100 IF (ERR = 155%) THEN RESUME 1210 ELSE ON ERROR GOTO 0
1120                                                         REM
1200                                                         REM
1210 PRINT \ PRINT "Part number does not exist"
1220          INPUT "Is it a new number (Y/N) ? = = > "; ANS$
1230             IF ANS$ = "Y" THEN PRINT "Use option 3" \ &
                    GOTO 610 ELSE PRINT "Incorrect number" \ &
                                 GOTO 520
1400                                                         REM
1410 CLOSE #1
1420 END
```

VI.C   REVIEW QUESTIONS

1. Compare the logical formats of sequential and relative files. What are the similarities and differences?
2. Do disk operating systems necessarily store data in relative files relative to the beginning of the file? Why is it useful to undertstand the difference between logical and physical

storage of data? How could this difference affect the use of relative keys?

3. If both sequential and relative files can be processed sequentially and randomly, what are the differences in applications? When would one be of advantage over the other?

4. Give a concise explanation of the use of *relative keys* in processing relative files. What is a key? How is it established? What would happen if a key to a particular record were forgotten?

5. What is meant by *hash coding*? When might it be used? On modern disk systems, is it usually the best system?

6. Compare the uses of *static* and *dynamic* buffering. Under what conditions might each be used?

VI.D   EXERCISES

1. Using the sample program as a guide, write and test a program to maintain an instructor's grade book. Student names are entered into the grade book alphabetically and numbered from one to however many students are in the class. The relative number for each student is the record key. Be sure the record layout contains a field for each column in the proposed grade book.

2. A high school English teacher wants a vocabulary drill developed for students wishing practice in taking college entrance examinations. Two students can develop and complete the project. Each can design, write, and test one of the programs. Care must be taken to ensure that record formats, etc., agree from the first program to the second. The completed project will need a set of complete instructions (with diagrams, if necessary) for the instructor.

    a. The first program permits the teacher to enter the drills, and then later make any necessary changes. The following format might be used for storing the drills. Records are to be stored in a relative file.

word form	choice 1	choice 2	choice 3	answer
scowl	boat	skull	look	look
concoct	destroy	prepare	ignore	prepare

The first record might also be reserved to hold the number of words available.

2					Record 1

b. The second program is to

(1) Read the number of words available (record 1)

(2) Randomly retrieve a word from the relative file

(3) Display the word and choices

(4) Get the student answers

If the answer is correct, a positive response is given (extra credit if selected from an array of possible responses).

If the answer is incorrect, the correct answer is displayed (extra credit is given if the correct answer is displayed in a reverse image field).

(5) At end of run, a total score is given

'n correct out of nn'

Care should be taken that all external and internal documentation is neat, accurate, and complete. Also, remember that someone is expected to use the results of this project. Ease of use and clarity are important.

VII
Indexed Files

VII.A PHYSICAL ORGANIZATION

Whether writing programs for microcomputers or for mainframe processing, the student programmer should learn to create and maintain indexed files as early as possible. These files are of extreme importance in an information and data system for randomly retrieving and updating records, especially when processing data interactively.

This chapter presents an overview of indexed files. The examples are kept short and easy to understand, but the processes they initiate and control are often quite complex.

VII.A.1 Indexed vs. Sequential and Relative Files

In contrast to sequential files, where records are retrieved in the order in which they were stored, records stored in indexed files are retrieved by the value of a key. Any record in an indexed file may be retrieved without examining the contents of another record.

In contrast to relative files where the keys represent logical distances of cells from the beginning of the file, keys for indexed files are stored in indexes along with the physical address of the record. The value of the key is supplied to the system, the key is located in an index, and the record address stored with the key is used to locate and retrieve a copy of the contents of the record.

Indexed files must consist of at least two files: one for the data records and one for the key/address records.

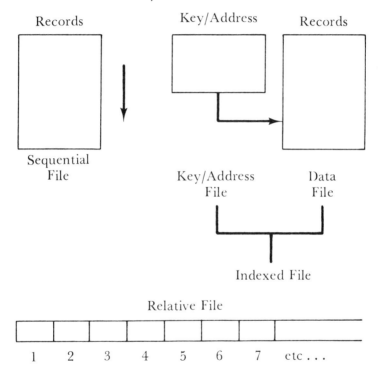

Sequential files are both physically and logically the same. Relative files store data in cells that are logically related one to another. Indexed files are maintained logically within an index (key/address) file, while the actual physical location of the data records is left to the resources of the system.

There are also other distinct differences among sequential, relative, and indexed files. Sequential files can be truncated, but individual records cannot be deleted from within a file. Records can be flagged as inactive, but not deleted. In the case of relative files, records are deleted by removing data from a cell or otherwise causing the cell to become empty. With indexed files, individual records may be logically deleted by simply removing the key and the corresponding address from the index file. The space used by the data record is then eventually released by the system for reuse.

Conversely, adding records to a sequential file means appending records to the file. Relative records are placed in empty cells. If all the cells are full, then the permissible number of keys must be increased. Indexed files permit data records to be logically inserted anywhere within the file, with corresponding changes to the index. Again, the actual physical location of the data record is left to the system.

VII.A.2 Keys

One other important difference—most systems do not permit more than one key to a file except for indexed files. Since keys for relative files are only logical locations of cells, these keys are not necessarily placed within the record. Keys for indexed files are always fields within the record, and there may be more than one key field. *Indexed files can be searched by single or multiple keys.* It is this property of indexed files that offers many of the options needed for information processing systems. It should also be remembered that relative keys do not necessarily provide true sequential access to records. Indexed keys are kept in lists, which permit sequential processing—often in both ascending and descending order.

VII.A.2.a Unique/Primary Keys

Primary keys are use to locate records stored in indexed files. *The key must be physically present in the record and its value must be unique.* "Physically present" means it is a field within the record, and "unique" means that no two keys may have the same value. And while records may be added or deleted within the file (thus adding or removing a value), key values themselves are normally not changed when contents of other fields are changed. On some systems, there exists the potential for contradictions between the index file and the data file.

VIII.A.2.b Alternate/Secondary Keys

Other data fields within the record may also be used as key fields. These keys are always in addition to the primary key. They can be used as alternate access routes for retrieving records. Since alternate keys are not the primary key, they are governed by other rules. Alternate keys do not have to be unique, their values may be updated, and they are treated differently by the system.

Keys

PRIMARY	ALTERNATE
1. Must be a field within a record	1. Must be a field within a record
2. Must have a unique value	2. Primary key must also exist
3. Only one primary key per file	3. May have more than one alternate key
4. Normally, no changes via updating	4. Values may be updated
	5. Keys may have duplicate values

Searching and retrieving data via keys is termed *random access*. The order in which the data is retrieved is dictated by circumstances outside the system, rather than by physical location within the file. There is, of course, an increase in system overhead when keys are created and maintained, but many modern operating systems are developed in anticipation of interactive data applications. Probably the most significant trade is that of need and usage vs. system load —and today the former usually wins. It should also be remembered that the system itself has a means of storing and locating data— quite separate from our understanding of file operations. Very often indexed files mesh extremely well with these systems.

VII.A.3 ISAM Files

ISAM stands for *Indexed Sequential Access Method*. It is a generic name for indexed files that can be processed both randomly and sequentially. This is made possible because key values, once established, are sorted (or otherwise ordered) before they are stored in the index files (see the next chapter).

The index file may be searched for a particular value and the corresponding address of the record located. The index may also be simply processed from beginning to end in sequential order. Records are not located by the order in which they were written, but rather sequentially by the (organized) values of the key. The ability to process data using several retrieval methods, as well as through several different paths, offers the additional advantage of letting the application dictate an access method, rather than the order of storage.

VII.A.4 Disk Storage

ISAM files are stored on disks or on diskettes because these storage media offer both random and sequential processing capabilities.

Data items are stored in sectors, which are logical and physical segments of tracks; and a predetermined number of tracks are available on each side of the disk(ette).

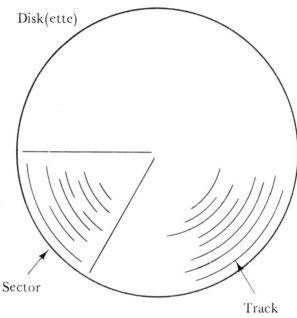

An address is the physical location of a piece of data or the beginning of a record. In many cases, it indicates the sector in which the data (or record) is stored. For example, an address might be composed of a combination of the number of the side of the disk (of part of a disk pack) where the sector is to be found, the track on which the sector is located, and the number of the sector.

$$\text{Address} = \text{disk} + \text{track} + \text{sector}$$
$$1008905 = 10 + 089 + 05$$

Actual addresses are, of course, more complicated, but this example illustrates the process.

VII.B CREATING AN INDEXED FILE: PUT

When creating indexed files, several rules must be remembered:

1. Keys must be a field within the record.
2. Primary key values must always be unique.

3. Records must first be sorted in ascending sequence according to the values of the key.

In contrast to sequential files where data may simply be typed into a file (FIFO), indexed files need a program to accept the data and create the necessary indexes. This is necessary because each indexed file must also have an accompanying file containing keys and record addresses. On many systems, the index file may not be listed in the file directory, but it exists nonetheless—and must at some point be created.

VII.B.1   Single (Primary) Keys

The following program example contains data to be stored in an indexed file. The primary key is the social security number.

174-82-6993	Ray Aldrich	12 Walker St.	Pon. MI	15206
773-38-1644	Mary Johnson	16 Aimes Ave.	Cols. OH	24608
686-14-1926	John Lockson	129 Oak Rd.	Det. MI	39617
173-37-1784	Jim Anderson	12 Vine St.	Cols. OH	24608
169-38-7736	Sam Samuals	114 King St.	Cols. OH	24608
782-56-7867	Sue Marion	14 Market St.	Pon. MI	15206
469-34-1487	Debbie King	15 Main St.	Pon. MI	15206

These data items must first be SORTED into ascending order, using the primary key field as the primary sort field. This may be done using a utility program, manually if on cards, or by writing a program.
The result:

169-38-7736	Sam Samuals	114 Kings Rd.	Cols. OH	24608
173-37-1784	Jim Anderson	...		
174-82-6993	Ray Aldrich	..		
469-34-1487	Debbie King	.		
686-14-1926	John Lockson			
773-38-1644	Mary Johnson			
782-56-7867	Sue Marion			

In the following program, the data are entered manually through a terminal as requested by the program. The indexed file will be called "INDFIL.DAT".

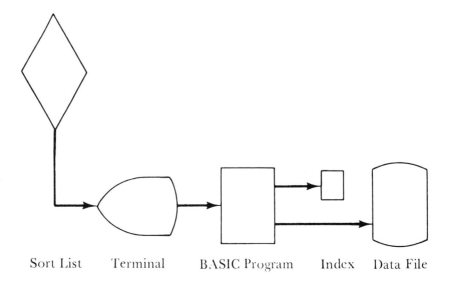

Sort List   Terminal   BASIC Program   Index   Data File

The record layout with variable names:

File Name: INDFIL.DAT
Key: SOC_SEC
Organization: Indexed-sequential

SOC_SEC	AN	9	social security number
NAME	AN	20	
ADDRESS	AN	20	
CITY_STATE	AN	10	
ZIP	N	5	

and the corresponding MAP statement:

```
100 MAP (INDSRC)     SOC_SEC$       =    9   &
                    , NAME$          =   20   &
                    , ADDRESS$       =   20   &
                    , CITY_STATE$    =   10   &
                    , ZIP%
```

The file organization (INDEXED) and the primary key (SOC_SEC) are identified in the OPEN statement and tied to a field in the MAP statement.

```
200 OPEN   'INDFIL.DAT' FOR OUTPUT AS FILE #1  &
           , ORGANIZATION INDEXED              &
           , PRIMARY KEY SOC__SEC$             &
           , MAP INDSRC
```

After the MAP and OPEN statements are written, the rest of the program can be completed. As the data is PUT to the disk, BASIC will create and manage the files.

When the data file is CLOSEd, the index will automatically be closed and stored for future reference.

PUT and the channel number are used to store the record.

```
ln PUT #n
```

```
500 PUT #1
```

Since records are stored logically in ascending order by the value of the key, it is not necessary to indicate a location for the key or the record. If the key value already exists, the error "Duplicate Key" is returned.

In the following program, note the ERROR statements. They are included to catch errors in sorting that would cause a primary key value to occur out of sequence, or in case a duplicate value were entered for a primary key. In such cases, an error message will be printed on the terminal, but the records would not be added to the file!

The program is terminated by entering a "0" when a prompt is given for a new social security number.

```
100 MAP (INDSRC)    SOC__SEC$     =    9   &
                    , NAME$       =   20   &
                    , ADDRESS$    =   20   &
                    , CITY__STATE$ =  10   &
                    , ZIP%
150                                                        REM
200 OPEN 'INDFIL.DAT' FOR OUTPUT AS FILE #1      &
             , ORGANIZATION INDEXED              &
             , PRIMAY KEY SOC__SEC$              &
             , MAP INDSRC
250                                                        REM
300 ON ERROR GOTO 710
350                                                        REM
400 INPUT "SOCIAL SECURITY NUMBER (0) = = > "; SOC__SEC$
410      IF SOC__SEC$ = "0" THEN 900
420 INPUT "NAME            = = > "; NAME$
```

```
430 INPUT "STREET          = => "; STREET$
440 LINPUT "CITY, STATE     = => "; CITY_STATE$
450 INPUT "ZIP              = => "; ZIP
475                                                          REM
500 PUT #1 \ GOTO 400
550                                                          REM
710 IF (ERR = 134%) AND (ERL = 500) THEN RESUME 800 &
      ELSE IF (ERR = 158%) AND (ERL = 500 ) THEN RESUME 850 &
      ELSE ON ERROR GOTO 0
750                                                          REM
800 PRINT "SOC-SEC NUMBER ALREADY EXISTS" \ GOTO 400
850 PRINT "SOC-SEC OUT OF SEQUENCE"        \ GOTO 400
875                                                          REM
900 CLOSE #1
950 END
```

VII.B.2   Multiple (Alternate) Keys

ISAM files with alternate key fields are created by adding an
ALTERNATE KEY option to the OPEN statement. For the sample
program above, the alternate key will be assumed to be the zip code.

```
100 OPEN 'INDFIL' FOR OUTPUT AS FILE #1      &
                , ORGANIZATION INDEXED        &
                , PRIMARY KEY SOC_SEC$        &
                , ALTERNATE KEY ZIP%          &
                    DUPLICATES               &
                    CHANGES                  &
                , MAP INSRC
```

BASIC assumes that key fields do not have duplicate values. If keys
are to have duplicate values, then the DUPLICATE parameter must
be added to the alternate key option. Unless this is done, BASIC
will check for duplicate values and generate an ERROR condition
if any duplicates are encountered.

This is also true for changing key values. Unless specified
in the OPEN statement, changes cannot be made to key values.
Attempts to do so will also cause an ERROR condition. If the
parameter CHANGES is included in the OPEN statement, then
values may be changed.

Once DUPLICATE and/or CHANGES is specified, BASIC
will automatically build the necessary indices and files. Remember,
however, that each option and parameter included in the OPEN
statement will cause additional system overhead. Unnecessary keys,
therefore, should not be generated in order to make the best use
of system resources and storage space.

```
100 MAP (INDSRC)    SOC_SEC$      =    9  &
                  , NAME$         =   20  &
                  , ADDRESS$      =   20  &
                  , CITY_STATE$   =   10  &
                  , ZIP%
150                                                           REM
200 OPEN 'INDSRC' FOR OUTPUT AS FILE #1  &
                  , ORGANIZATION INDEXED    &
                  , PRIMARY KEY SOC_SEC$    &
                  , ALTERNATE KEY ZIP%      &
                       DUPLICATES           &
                       CHANGES              &
                  , MAP INDSRC
250                                                           REM
300 ON ERROR GOTO 710
350                                                           REM
400 INPUT "SOCIAL SECURITY NUMBER (0) = => "; SOC_SEC$
410      IF SOC_SEC$ =, "0" THEN 900
420 INPUT "NAME        = => "; NAME$
430 INPUT "STREET      = => "; STREET$
440 LINPUT "CITY, STATE = => "; CITY_STATE$
450 INPUT "ZIP         = => "; ZIP%
475                                                           REM
500 PUT #1  GOTO 400
500                                                           REM
710 IF (ERR = 134%) AD (ERL = 500%) THEN RESUME 800       &
    ELSE IF (ERR = 158%) AND (ERL = 500%) THEN RESUME 850   &
    ELSE ON ERROR GOTO 0
750                                                           REM
800 PRINT "SOC-SEC NUMBER ALREADY EXISTS" \ GOTO 400
850 PRINT "SOC-SEC OUT OF SEQUENCE"        \ GOTO 400
875                                                           REM
900 CLOSE #1
950 END
```

VII.B.3   Processing ISAM Records

In order to retrieve a record from storage, the GET command then retrieves a copy of the contents of the record. The difference between these two commands is that FIND locates the record and moves the record pointers, but it does not move a copy of the data into the input buffer. A successful execution of the FIND command indicates that a given record containing the specified key value exists. The actual operation required to move (copy) data is not envoked. GET can, however, be used to both locate and retrieve record contents. It is probably the command most often used for accessing ISAM files. But if one wants only to determine if a record exists before deleting it, then FIND might prove sufficient. But be careful to save needed data.

VII.B.3.a   Using Keys to Process ISAM Files

In the examples used so far in this chapter, there are two key fields: a primary key and one alternate key. BASIC references these keys by means of numbers. The primary key is called KEY 0%. Any alternate keys begin with KEY 1%, and continue with KEY 2%, KEY 3%, etc., for however many alternate keys have been declared in the OPEN statement.

For the OPEN statement:

```
200 OPEN 'INDSRC' FOR INPUT AS FILE #1          &
            , ORGANIZATION INDEXED               &
            , PRIMARY KEY SOC_SEC$               &
            , ALTERNATE KEY ZIP%                 &
                        DUPLICATES               &
                        CHANGES                  &
            , MAP INDSRC
```

the primary key SOC_SEC$ is referenced as KEY 0% and the alternate key becomes KEY 1%.

BASIC uses the following FIND and GET formats:

```
                        ┌────┐
                        │ EQ │
ln   FIND   #n   KEY #  │ GE │  STRING
     GET                │ GT │  INTER/VARIABLE
                        └────┘
```

(A):   400 FIND #1,   KEY 0%   EQ "686-14-1926"
          400 FIND #1,   KEY 1%   EQ 24608
          400 FIND #1,   KEY 1%   EQ ZIP_CODE%

(B):   400 GET #1, KEY 0% EQ "686-14-1926"
          400 GET #1, KEY 1% EQ 24608
          400 GET #1, KEY 1% EQ ZIP_CODE%

| KEY 0% = SOC_SEC$ | KEY 1% = ZIP% |

Whenever a match is not found for a key value, "Record not Found" is returned as the error message. When the GT expression is used, BASIC searches for a key with the next highest value. If none is found, an "End of File" message is returned.

VII.B.3.b Locating ISAM Records: FIND

FIND is used to determine the existence of a record with a given key value. It locates the record, but does not cause data to be moved.

To locate ISAM records sequentially (i.e., to move the current record pointer), simply use the FIND command and the channel number. This locates the record with the next highest key value *of the key last referenced* in a BASIC statement.

```
400 FIND #1
```

If the last key referenced had been the primary key, then this command would locate the next highest primary key. If the last key referenced, however, had been an alternate key, then BASIC would attempt to locate the next highest key value for that particular alternate key. Whenever no key has been previously specified in a BASIC program, the primary key is assumed.

To locate key values randomly (rather than sequentially), use one of the options described in the section above.

```
400 FIND #1 KEY 0% EQ "686-14-1926"
```

VII.B.3.c Retrieving ISAM Records: GET

To read ISAM read sequentially, GET is used with the assigned channel number.

```
400 GET #1
```

Each succesive GET locates the next highest key value *of the key last referenced*. The conventions for the GET statement are the same as those for FIND. Unless a key has been previously referenced, the primary key is assumed. If a key has been referenced in an earlier statement, it is then assumed to be the key referenced. An attempt will be made to locate the key with the next highest value.

When retrieving ISAM records randomly, GET is used with specified key values.

```
400 GET #1, KEY #1 EQ 24608
```

Here the record pointer will be set to the next record with an alternate key (ZIP%) value of 24608. Successive GETs would then continue to retrieve ZIP codes with this value, or until a "Record not Found" condition is returned.

VII.B.3.d   Modifying ISAM Records: UPDATE

Although it is possible on some BASIC systems to UPDATE values of primary keys, this is in general practice not a good idea. It is usually best to create and delete records when a primary field needs changing. The following examples assume that any field may be modified except the primary key field. To change values of alternate keys, CHANGES must also be specified in the OPEN statement.

Note also that an UPDATE command will not work unless a GET is first performed. ACCESS MODIFY should also be specified in the OPEN statement.

Once the contents of a record are moved (GET) into the I/O buffer area, any of its fields may be modified. The contents of the buffer are then rewritten to the same storage location where the original contents of the record were stored. This overwrites the storage location with a new record. [When primary keys are updated, a new record is usually created and the old one deleted.]

For example, to change the spelling of Debbie King in the data set used in the last chapter.

1. INPUT her social security number
2. GET a copy of the contents of the record [ERROR will occur if not found]
3. INPUT the new spelling
4. UPDATE (rewrite) the contents of the record

```
100 MAP (INDSRC)    SOC_SEC$     =    9  &
                    , NAME$       =   20  &
                    , ADDRESS$    =   20  &
                    , CITY_STATE$ =   10  &
                    , ZIP%

200 OPEN 'INDFIL.DAT' FOR INPUT AS FILE #1   &
              , ORGANIZATION INDEXED          &
              , ACCESS MODIFY                 &
              , PRIMARY KEY SOC_SEC$          &
              , ALTERNATE KEY ZIP%            &
              , MAP INDSRC
300                                                         REM
400 ON ERROR GOTO . . . . .
450                                                         REM
500 INPUT "SOCIAL SECURITY NUMBER (0) = = > "; SS_NUMBER$
550      IF SS_NUMBER$ = "0" THEN . . . . .
600 GET #1, KEY 0% = SS_NUMBER$
650                                                         REM
```

```
 700 PRINT NAME$, ADDRESS$, CITY_STATE$, ZIP%
 750 PRINT "Is this the correct record (Y/N) = = > "; ANS$
 800     IF ANS$ <> "Y" THEN 500
 850                                                        REM
 900 INPUT "Enter New Spelling = = > "; NAME$
 950                                                        REM
1000 UPDATE #1    \      GOTO 500
```

This sample does not include specific error routines or the ability to make changes to other data fields in the record. The one change that can be made is in line 900. Once NAME$ is INPUT as a new value, this value automatically becomes the new value of the NAME$ field in the buffer. Thus, when the UPDATE command is executed, it need only contain a reference to channel #1. The key is not specified because the GET in line 600 left the current record pointer at the record last read into memory. The UPDATE command rewrites the contents of this record.

VII.B.3.e   Deleting ISAM Records: DELETE

The DELETE command works in much the same manner as UPDATE. It is only necessary to issue a FIND to move the current record pointer to the record to be deleted. A successful FIND also indicates that the record exists. DELETE and the channel number then remove the record from the index.

```
400 DELETE #1
```

Note, however, that simply using FIND and DELETE does not mean that the *logically correct* record has been found—only a record with a matching key!
Without proper care, needed data may be destroyed.
It is best to issue a GET and make sure that the correct data record has been located before a DELETE command is executed.

```
1250 INPUT "ENTER SOCIAL SECURITY NUMBER (0) = = > "; SS_NUMBER$
       . . .
1400 GET #1, KEY 0% EQ SS_NUMBER$
       . . .
1500 PRINT NAME$, ADDRESS$, CITY_STATE$, ZIP%
1550 PRINT "Is this the information to be removed? = = > "; ANS$
1600     IF ANS$ <> "Y" THEN . . . .
       . . .
1900 DELETE #1
```

In a data or information system, DELETE should be used with great care. Failure to do so may cause hours of difficult work restoring files and their contents.

VII.B.3.f Restoring ISAM Keys: RESTORE

The RESTORE command is used to move the current record pointer to the beginning of the file. When successive FIND or GET commands are issued, BASIC works sequentially through the records stored in a file. Each new FIND or GET (without KEY values) begins at the current point and moves forward in the files. Should the needed record be located before the actual location of the current record pointer, however, it is then necessary to move the current pointer to a point before the needed record.

RESTORE used by itself restores the key last referenced in the program. When used with a key, it restores the key named in the statement.

400 RESTORE #1

> [Sets the record pointer to the
> beginning of the file, using
> the key last referenced]

400 RESTORE #1, KEY 0%

> [Sets the record pointer to the
> beginning of the file, using
> the primary key]

NOTE: The RESTORE command is used to relocate a record pointer for a particular key to the beginning of the file. It does not change keys. Use the FIND or the GET command with the KEY needed to change KEYs.

400 FIND #1, KEY 0%

This example sets the key pointer to the primary key. The RESTORE command does not by itself change the key currently being used in the program.

VII.B.4 Sample Program

The following program maintains a small inventory in the form of an address book.

Note how the use of ERROR routines save programming time and effort.

```
   5 ON ERROR GOTO 9000
  10                                                              REM
  20 REM        INDEXED SEQUENTIAL MAINTENANCE
  30                                                              REM
  40 REM     THIS PROGRAM MAINTAINS AN INDEXED
  50 REM     SEQUENTIAL FILE CALLED 'MASTER.DAT'
  60                                                              REM

 100 MAP (MASTER)     ID$        =    9                    &
                     , NAME$     =   25                    &
                     , ADDRESS$  =   20                    &
                     , CITY$     =   15                    &
                     , STATE$    =    2                    &
                     , ZIP%
 150                                                              REM
 200 OPEN 'MASTER.DAT' FOR INPUT AS FILE #1             &
          , ORGANIZATION INDEXED                        &
          , PRIMARY KEY ID$                             &
          , ACCESS MODIFY                               &
          , MAP MASTER
 250                                                              REM
 300 PRINT \ PRINT "Select one of the following options" \ PRINT
 310 PRINT "          1- Inquiry          3- Delete"
 320 PRINT "          2- Add              4- Change"
 335 PRINT "                    5 = End"
 340 PRINT \ INPUT "          Enter option = => "; OPT%
 350    IF OPT% > 5 THEN PRINT "Incorrect entry" \ GOTO 300
 360    ON OPT% GOTO 1000, 2000, 3000, 4000, 9990
 370 REM                                                         REM
1000 REM ***********************************************
1010 REM *                                             *
1020 REM *   1000 = Inquiry only                       *
1030 REM *                                             *
1040 REM ***********************************************
1050                                                             REM
1100 PRINT \ PRINT "Enter ID-Code (9 digits) = => " ; ID$
1110 GET #1, KEY #0 EQ ID$
1120                                                             REM
1130 PRINT \ PRINT "    ID-Code        "; ID$ \ PRINT
1140 PRINT "    NAME           "; NAME$
1150 PRINT "    ADDRESS        "; ADDRESS$
1160 PRINT "    CITY           "; CITY$
1170 PRINT "    STATE          "; STATE$
1180 PRINT "    ZIP CODE       "; ZIP%
1190                                                             REM
1200 INPUT "Continue (Y/N) "; ANS$
1210    IF MID$(ANS$, 1, 1) = "Y" THEN 300 ELSE 9990
1220                                                             REM
```

```
2000 REM ************************************************
2010 REM *                                               *
2020 REM *      2000 = Add records                        *
2030 REM *                                               *
2040 REM ************************************************
2050                                                            REM

2100 INPUT "ID-Code        = "; ID$
2110 INPUT "NAME           = "; NAME$
2120 INPUT "ADDRESS        = "; ADDRESS$
2130 INPUT "CITY           = "; CITY$
2140 INPUT "STATE          = "; STATE$
2150 INPUT "ZIP CODE       = "; ZIP%

2160                                                            REM
2200 PRINT \ PRINT
2210 INPUT "Keep this information (Y/N) "; ANS$
2220    IF MID$ (ANS$, 1, 1) <> "Y" THEN 2240
2230 PUT #1
2235                                                            REM
2240 PRINT \ INPUT "Add another (Y/N) "; ANS$
2250    IF MID$ (ANS$, 1, 1) = "Y" THEN 2100
2260 INPUT "Continue (Y/N) "; ANS$
2270    IF MID$ (ANS$, 1, 1) = "Y" THEN 300 ELSE 9990
2280                                                            REM
3000 REM ************************************************
3010 REM *                                               *
3020 REM *      3000 = Delete a record                    *
3030 REM *                                               *
3040 REM ************************************************
3050                                                            REM
3100 PRINT \ PRINT
3110 INPUT "Enter ID-Code (9 digits) "; ID$
3120 GET #1, KEY 0% EQ ID$
3130                                                            REM
3140 PRINT \ PRINT
3150 PRINT NAME$, ADDRESS$
3160 PRINT CITY$, STATE$, ZIP%
3170 PRINT
3180 INPUT "Is this the information to be deleted (Y/N) "; ANS$
3190    IF MID$ (ANS$, 1, 1) <> "Y" THEN 3300
3200 DELETE #1
3210 PRINT \ PRINT "Information deleted" \ PRINT
3220                                                            REM
3300 INPUT "Delete another (Y/N) "; ANS$
3310    IF MID$ (ANS$, 1, 1) = "Y" THEN 3100
3320 INPUT "Continue (Y/N) "; ANS$
3330    IF MIS$ (ANS$, 1, 1) = "Y" THEN 300 ELSE 9990
3340                                                            REM
```

```
4000 REM ***************************************************
4010 REM *                                                 *
4020 REM *       4000 = Update record or field             *
4030 REM *                                                 *
4040 REM ***************************************************
4050                                                     REM
4100 PRINT \ PRINT
4110 INPUT "Enter ID-Code (9 digits) "; ID$
4120 GET #1, KEY 0 EQ ID$
4130                                                     REM
4140 PRINT \ PRINT
4150 PRINT NAME$, ADDRESS$
4160 PRINT CITY$, STATE$, ZIP%
4170 PRINT
4180                                                     REM
4200 PRINT "Select number of data to be changed"
4210 PRINT "     1- all        3- address      4- state"
4220 PRINT "     2- name       4- city         6- zip code"
4230 PRINT
4240 INPUT "                    7- No (other) changes  ==> "; OPT%
4250    IF OPT% > 8 THEN PRINT "Incorrect number\" \ GOTO 4140
4260 ON OPT% GOTO 4400, 4400, 4410, 4420, 4430, 4440, 4450
4270                                                     REM
4400 INPUT "NAME      = "; NAME$      \ IF OPT% > 1 THEN 4140
4410 INPUT "ADDRESS   = "; ADDRESS"   \ IF OPT% > 1 THEN 4140
4420 INPUT "CITY      = "; CITY$      \ IF OPT% > 1 THEN 4140
4430 INPUT "STATE     = "; STATE"     \ IF OPT% > 1 THEN 4140
4440 INPUT "ZIP CODE  = "; ZIP%       \ GOTO 4140
4445                                                     REM
4450 UPDATE #1
4500                                                     REM
4510 INPUT "Change another (Y/N) "; ANS$
4520    IF MID$ (ANS$, 1, 1) = "Y" THEN 4100
4530 INPUT "Continue (Y/N) "; ANS$
4540    IF MID$ (ANS$, 1, 1) = "Y" THEN 300 ELSE 9990
```

```
8000 REM *********************************************
8010 REM *                                           *
8020 REM *       9000 = ERROR and CLOSE routines      *
8030 REM *                                           *
8040 REM *********************************************
8050                                               REM
9000 RESUME 9100
9010                                               REM
9100 IF (ERR = 5%)                                  &
         THEN PRINT \ PRINT "MASTER FILE NOT AVAILABLE" \  &
         GOTO 9999                                  &
       ELSE IF (ERR = 134%)                         &
         THEN PRINT \ PRINT "ID-Code ALREADY EXISTS" \  &
         GOTO 300                                   &
       ELSE IF (ERR = 155%)                         &
         THEN PRINT \ PRINT "ID-Code DOES NOT EXIST" \  &
         GOTO 300                                   &
       ELSE                                         &
         PRINT \ PRINT ERL; " "; ERT$ (ERR); " "; ERR
9500                                               REM
9990 CLOSE #1
9999 END
```

VII.C REVIEW QUESTIONS

1. Compare the logical format of indexed files with those of sequential and relative files. Why do indexed files have two files? Who creates and maintains these files?

2. If sequential and relative records are not stored contiguously on your system, are they indexed by the system?

3. How are relative keys different from index keys?

4. What are primary keys and secondary keys? Who decides which are which?

5. Is it important to consider which keys might be changed more often, and which hardly ever?

6. Explain how disk(ette)s are used to store data.

7. What are addresses, sectors, and tracks? How many records can be stored on a sector?

8. How many bytes per sector on your disk system? How much data will your disk system store?

VII.D EXERCISES

1. Modify the sample program to process an alternate key using the zip code. Then open the file for OUTPUT and create a test data file.

2. Write a program to prepare address labels upon request by zip code. Use the test data file created above or one supplied by your instructor.

3. A record mart in the local shopping center needs a program to organize and control its inventory. The design of the program calls for an indexed file, with the record I.D. number to serve as the primary key. Secondary keys are to be created for the media (tape, lps, etc.) and the genre (country/western, classical, etc.). A quick trip to a record store might also be helpful. This project can be completed by four students: one for each of the three main programs, and one to prepare the test data and the user's manual.

ID	Singer/group	Title	Media	Genre	Value
46-1072	Rogers, Buck	Greatest Hits	T	C/W	5.99

a. Design a system flowchart and a record layout for this project. Design the necessary codes. Set up procedures to prevent loss of data.

b. Using the steps suggested in exercise 4 of Chapter V, write and test a program to maintain (display, add, delete, and modify) the indexed file.

c. Write and test a program to print a report with subtotals and grand total by genre.

d. Write and test a program to print a report with subtotals and grand total by medium.

e. Carefully document each program and prepare a short but clearly written user manual.

VIII
Linked Lists

VIII.A   LINKED LISTS

The following two chapters assume a working knowledge of tables and arrays.

A review of the examples in Chapter II might be helpful at this point.

Linked lists are used to represent complex data structures and are of special relevance to many networks and data bases using hierarchical and relational structuring. This chapter and the next (inverted lists) present a bridge to data base processing. Also of interest in these two chapters will be the use of linked lists to handle primary keys and inverted lists for storing secondary keys. In many ways, the ability to efficiently manage relationships among data items begins with an understanding of linked lists. Once the concept of a linked list is mastered, the door to more complex data structures is wide open.

A *list* is little more than a group of ordered data elements or items; and a *link* is pointer to the next data element. A *linked list* is then a group of data items, which are kept in (logical) order by means of pointers from one item to another.

Linked lists are represented in programs by means of arrays and subscripts. For example, a two-dimensional array can be constructed to contain both the data item and the pointers (or links). If the data items are called "A", "M", and "Z", then:

	Link	Data Item		Link	Data Item
Head = 1	2	A	Head = 2	3	M
	3	M		1	A
	0	Z		0	Z

In the first array, the HEAD points to row 1 (or the letter A). The link (pointer) in column 1 of row 1 in turn points to the next data item (the letter M and row 2). And the link in column 1 of row 2 points to the next item, which is in row 3 (or the letter Z).

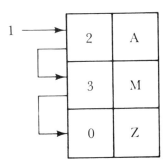

NOTE: For the sake of simplicity, "A", "M", and "Z" may be considered single data items, record addresses, or stored keys.

In the second array, the links go from the head to row 2; from row 2 to row 1; and from row 1 to row 3.

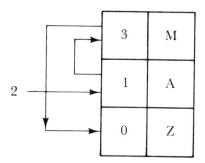

In BASIC, the list can be printed by using a CURRENT_PTR to indicate which row is currently being referenced. For programming convenience, column 1 will be called the link, or NEXT_PTR. Column 2 will contain the data item, or the STORED_KEY. We will assume that the array contains three items (USED = 3).

CURRENT_PTR = HEAD \ NEXT_PTR = 1 \ STORED_KEY = 2

```
      FOR NEXT_ITEM = 1 TO USED
          PRINT ARRAY (CURRENT_PTR, STORED_KEY)
          CURRENT_PTR = ARRAY (CURRENT_PTR, NEXT_PTR)
      NEXT NEXT_ITEM
```

VIII.A.1 Adding to Linked Lists

It is not necessary to move data items when new data items are to be added to the list. The new item is added at the bottom and two links are reset. To insert a "D", the letter is added a the bottom. The link from "A" is changed to the position of "D", and "D" then assumes the link to "M".

HEAD = 2
USED = 3

3	M
1	A
0	Z
0	0

Before

HEAD = 2
USED = 4

3	M
4	A
0	Z
1	D

After

The result is:

$$\text{"A"} \qquad \text{"D"} \qquad \text{"M"} \qquad \text{"Z"}$$

or:

from 2 to 4 to 1 to 3—and the end

Note the difference between the logical and the physical locations of the data items.

In BASIC, it is necessary to first find a free slot (or row) before the data item can be entered and the links reset.

```
NEXT_PTR = 1 \ STORED_KEY = 2 \ USED = 3

    FOR FREE_SLOT = 1 TO ARRAY_SIZE
        IF ARRAY (FREE_SLOT, STORED_KEY) = 0 THEN GOTO . . . . . .
    NEXT FREE_SLOT
```

(Result: FREE_SLOT = 4)

Next, find the logical order of the item in the list. NEW_ITEM is given the value "D".   Note the use of a PREVIOUS_PTR in the example.

```
CURRENT_PTR = HEAD

FOR SEARCH = 1 TO USED
    IF NEW_ITEM < ARRAY (CURRENT_PTR, STORED_KEY) THEN GOTO . .
    PREVIOUS_PTR = CURRENT_PTR
    CURRENT_PTR = ARRAY (CURRENT_PTR, NEXT_PTR)
NEXT SEARCH
```

(Result: PREVIOUS_PTR = 2, CURRENT_PTR = 1)

HEAD = 2   \   USED = 3   \   NEW_ITEM = D

CURRENT_PTR	3	M
PREVIOUS_PTR	1	A
	0	Z
FREE_SLOT	0	0

   At this point, the CURRENT_PTR will point to the first data
item larger than our NEW_ITEM; and the PREVIOUS_PTR will
point to the largest data item that is smaller than our NEW_ITEM.
The data can now be moved to accommodate the new data item.

ARRAY (NEW_SLOT, STORED_KEY) = NEW_ITEM   or: ARRAY (4, 2) = D
ARRAY (NEW_SLOT, NEXT_PTR) = CURRENT_PTR   ARRAY (4, 1) = 1
ARRAY (PREVIOUS_PTR, NEXT_PTR) = NEW_SLOT   ARRAY (2, 1) = 4

USED = USED + 1

HEAD = 1 \   USED = 3   HEAD = 2 \   USED = 4

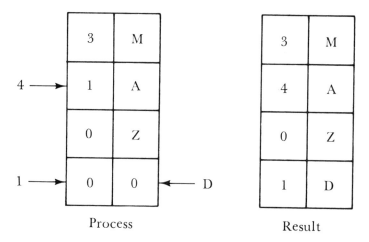

              Process   Result

   The advantage of using linked lists is that data items can be
added or deleted from a list without disturbing any of the other
data items. When using indexed sequential files, either the primary
indices must be sorted before processing sequentially, or another
method of handling the indices must be used. Linked lists provide
a good method for processing primary keys in indices. Sorting
large indices can use a lot of system overhead and cause delays in
response and retrieval times.
   There are, of course, some disadvantages as there always are
in any computer routine. Space is needed for the arrays (or links).
Random retrieval can also be slow when large lists are searched. In
a sequential file, it is sometimes possible to position more commonly
used data items at the top of the file, and thus save processing time.
But on the whole, linked lists provide a fast means for finding data
items. And, once one is familiar with the processes involved, other
more complex structures are easier to handle.

VIII.A.1.a Single Linked Lists

When developing programs for linked lists, there are basically three considerations that determine the flow of the program:

1. If the array is empty—i.e., without data items—then the HEAD must be set, and the data item entered.
2. If the data item is to be inserted logically somewhere *within* the list or is to be added logically to the *end* of the list, then the relevant links must be changed and the data items entered.
3. If the data item is to be added to the *beginning* of the list, then the HEAD must be reset, the relevant links added, and the data item entered.

It is also necessary to check for error conditions. For example:

1. Is the new data item already in the list?
2. Is there room in the array for new items?

The following example should be studied carefully. It can be used to establish a linked list, and then to add more keys. Row 0 is used to store the location of the HEAD and the number of rows USED.

Array   =   IND(6,2) \   SIZE = 6 (rows)

Row 0   =   a storage row
            IND(STORAGE,HEAD) = IND(0,1)
            IND(STORAGE,USED) = IND(0,2)

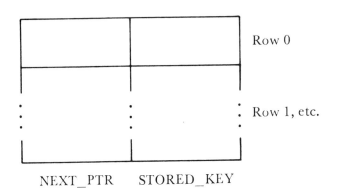

NEXT_PTR   STORED_KEY

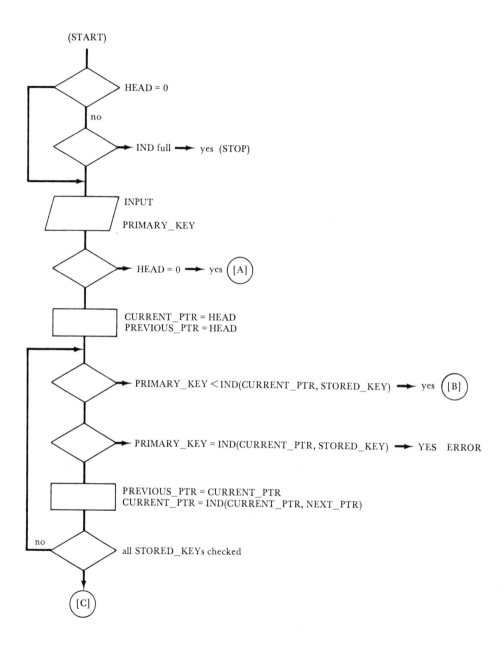

NOTE: For the sake of this example, keys will be assumed to be integers.

In BASIC:

```
*********** set values for variables ***************

STORAGE = 0 \ HEAD = 1 \ USED = 2
NEXT_PTR = 1 \ STORED_KEY = 2
DIM IND(6,2) \ SIZE = 6

*********** check if array is full ****************

IF IND(STORAGE,HEAD) = 0 THEN 1000                        &
    ELSE IF IND(STORAGE,USED) = SIZE                      &
         THEN PRINT "INDEX FULL" \ GOTO [STOP]


**********************************************************
*                                                        *
  [A] = Array is empty
  [B] = Insert primary key at beginning or within list
  [C] = Enter key at end of list
*                                                        *
**********************************************************

1000 INPUT "Enter primary key ==> "; PRIMARY_KEY
     IF IND(STORAGE,HEAD) = 0 THEN .. [A]

     CURRENT_PTR = IND(STORAGE,HEAD)
     PREVIOUS_PTR = IND(STORAGE,HEAD)

     FOR SEARCH = 1 TO IND(STORAGE,USED)
         IF PRIMARY_KEY < IND(CURRENT,STORED_KEY) THEN .. [B]
         IF PRIMARY_KEY = IND(CURRENT_PTR,STORED_KEY)          &
            THEN PRINT "Duplicate key" \ GOTO .. [STOP]
         PREVIOUS_PTR = CURRENT_PTR
         CURRENT_PTR = IND(CURRENT_PTR,NEXT_PTR)
     NEXT SEARCH
     .
     .
     .
    (C)

    .. (A) ..
```

If HEAD = 0, then the array is presumed to be empty.

```
IND(1,STORED_KEY)       = PRIMARY_KEY
IND(1,NEXT_PTR)         = 0
IND(STORAGE,HEAD)       = 1
IND(STORAGE,USED)       = IND(STORAGE,USED) + 1
```

Before any further data items can be added to the list, it is necessary to formulate a subroutine to find empty cells in the array. When a list is first created, the cells are obviously all empty and the data items could simply be stored. This would not be true, however, if the array had already been used, with data items added and deleted. A small subroutine is written to find the first empty cell. They are assumed to contain zeros.

```
4950 FOR NEW_SLOT = 1 TO SIZE
       IF IND (STORAGE, USED) = SIZE THEN PRINT "Index Full" [STOP
       IF IND (NEW_SLOT, STORED_KEY) = 0 THEN RETURN
       NEXT NEW_SLOT
       .. (B) ..
```

The primary key is to be inserted into the list, either at the beginning or within the list, but not at the end.

```
GOSUB 4950          ! GET EMPTY CELL

IND (NEW_SLOT, STORED_KEY)    = PRIMARY_KEY
IND (NEW_SLOT, NEXT_PTR)      = CURRENT_PTR
IND (STORAGE, USED)           = IND (STORAGE, USED) + 1
```

NOTE: If the primary key is to be inserted at the logical beginning of the list, then change HEAD; otherwise, change NEXT_PTR of next lowest STORED_KEY.

```
IF PRIMARY_KEY < IND (IND (STORAGE, HEAD), STORED-KEY)      &
   THEN IND (STORAGE, HEAD) = NEW_SLOT                      &
   ELSE IND (PREVIOUS_PTR, NEXT_PTR) = NEW_SLOT
```

.. (C) ..

The primary key is to be inserted at the logical end of the list.

```
GOSUB 4950          ! GET EMPTY CELL

IND (NEW_SLOT, STORED_KEY)    = PRIMARY_KEY
IND (NEW_SLOT, NEXT_PTR)      = 0
IND (PREVIOUS_PTR, NEXT_PTR)  = NEW_SLOT
IND (STORAGE, USED)           = IND (STORAGE, USED) + 1
```

To PRINT the list:

```
CURRENT_PTR = IND(STORAGE,HEAD)
FOR DA_TA = 1 TO IND(STORAGE,USED)
    PRINT IND(CURRENT_PTR,STORED_KEY),
    CURRENT_PTR = IND(CURRENT_PTR,NEXT_PTR)
NEXT DA_TA
PRINT
```

VIII.A.1.b   Multiple Linked Lists

In the examples above, the linked list is maintained in ascending order. The data items are logically stored and printed from the smallest data item to the largest. This arrangement, however, does not offer the possibility of processing the data items in another order—for example, in descending order. It would also be difficult to delete data items from the list.

In order to process data items in more than one order, more than one list is maintained. This, of course, creates a little more system overhead, but as will be seen in the next section, the actual process of adding and deleting data items can be done quickly and efficiently.

The following example creates a reverse linked list, and is then added to the routines described above. The data items can then be printed in both ascending and descending order.

	NEXT_PTR	STORED_KEY	REV_PTR
Head = 2	3	M	4
Tail = 3	4	A	0
	0	Z	1
	1	D	2

In this example, REV_PTR always indicates the next lowest key.

To PRINT the list in descending order, simply begin with the TAIL, and follow the REV_PTRs.

```
CURRENT_PTR = IND (STORAGE, TAIL)

FOR DA_TA = 1 TO IND (STORAGE, USED)
    PRINT IND (CURRENT_PTR, STORED_KEY) ,
    CURRENT_PTR = IND (CURRENT_PTR, REV_PTR)
NEXT DA_TA
PRINT
```

VIII.A.1.c Sample Program

This program will create and maintain a multiple linked list similar
to the one in the above example. The keys are to be numeric, and
the dimension of the array is increased to hold both sets of links.

Study this program carefully. Use your own arrays and data
items on scratch paper, and follow each step.

```
**************** set values for variables ************

50 DECLARE INTEGER PRIMARY_KEY, PREVIOUS_PTR, NEXT_PTR, STORED _KEY        &
                , STORAGE, HEAD, SIZE, USED, REV_PTR
100 NEXT_PTR = 1 \ STORED_KEY = 2 \ STORAGE = 0 \ HEAD = 1 \ TAIL = 2
110 USED = 3 \ REV_PTR = 3
150                                                              REM
200 DIM IND (6, 3) \ SIZE = 6
250                                                              REM

************* check if array empty ******************

4000 IF IND (STORAGE, HEAD) = 0 THEN 4100                                 &
        ELSE IF IND (STORAGE, USED) = SIZE THEN
                PRINT "Index Full" \ GOTO 9000
4010                                                             REM

  ***********************************************************
  *                                                         *
    4540 = Add at end of list

    4630 = Insert at beginning or within array

    4750 = Empty array

    4950 = Subroutine to find empty slot

  *                                                         *
  ***********************************************************

4100 PRINT "          "; \ INPUT "Enter primary key (0) = => "; PRIMARY_KEY
4150 PRINT
4200        IF PRIMARY_KEY = 0 THEN 9000
4250 IF IND (STORAGE, HEAD)   = 0 THEN 4750
4300 CURRENT_PTR = IND (STORAGE, HEAD) \ PREVIOUS_PTR = CURRENT_PTR
4400 FOR KEY_SEARCH = 1 TO IND (STORAGE, USED)
4410     IF PRIMARY_KEY < IND (CURRENT_PTR, STORED_KEY) THEN 4630
4420     IF PRIMARY_KEY = IND (CURRENT_PTR, STORED_KEY) &
                        THEN PRINT "DUPLICATE KEY" \ GOTO 4100
4430     PREVIOUS_PTR = CURRENT_PTR
4440     CURRENT_PTR = IND (CURRENT_PTR, NEXT_PTR)
4450 NEXT KEY_SEARCH
4490                                                             REM
```

```
************* Add to end of list ******************

4540 GOSUB 4950
4550      IND(NEW_SLOT,STORED_KEY) = PRIMARY_KEY
4560      IND(NEW_SLOT,NEXT_PTR)    = 0
4570      IND(PREVIOUS_PTR,NEXT_PTR) = NEW_SLOT
4572      IND(NEW_SLOT,REV_PTR) = IND(STORAGE,TAIL)
4576      IND(STORAGE,TAIL) = NEW_SLOT
4580      IND(STORAGE,USED) = IND(STORAGE,USED) + 1
4590 PRINT IND(0,1), IND(0,2), IND(0,3) \ PRINT
4592 MAT PRINT IND, \ PRINT \ GOTO 4100
4595                                                              REM


************* Insert at beginning or within list**

4630 GOSUB 4950
4640      IND(NEW_SLOT,STORED_KEY) = PRIMARY_KEY
4650      IND(NEW_SLOT,NEXT_PTR)    = CURRENT_PTR
4670      IND(STORAGE,USED) = IND(STORAGE,USED) + 1
4680      IF PRIMARY_KEY < IND(IND(STORAGE,HEAD),STORED_KEY)          &
              THEN IND(STORAGE,HEAD) = NEW_SLOT \                     &
                   IND(PREVIOUS_PTR,REV_PTR) = NEW_SLOT \             &
                   IND(NEW_SLOT,REV_PTR) = 0                          &
              ELSE IND(PREVIOUS_PTR,NEXT_PTR) = NEW_SLOT \            &
                   IND(NEW_SLOT,REV_PTR) = IND(CURRENT_PTR,REV_PTR) \ &
                   IND(CURRENT_PTR,REV_PTR) = NEW_SLOT
4690 PRINT IND(0,1), IND(0,2), IND(0,3) \ PRINT
4692 MAT PRINT IND, \ GOTO 4100
4695                                                              REM


************* Enter at end of list ***************

4750      IND(1,STORED_KEY) = PRIMARY_KEY
4760      IND(1,NEXT_PTR)    = 0
4780      IND(STORAGE,HEAD)  = 1
4782      IND(CURRENT_PTR,REV_PTR) = 0
4786  '   IND(STORAGE,TAIL)  = 1
4788      IND(STORAGE,USED) = IND(STORAGE,USED) + 1
4790 PRINT IND(0,1), IND(0,2), IND(0,3) \ PRINT
4792 MAT PRINT IND, \ PRINT \ GOTO 4100
4795                                                              REM
```

```
************* Subroutine for empty slot **********

4950 FOR SLOT = 1 TO SIZE
4955     IF SIZE = IND(STORAGE,USED) THEN PRINT "Index full " \ GOTO 4100
4960     IF IND(SLOT,STORED_KEY) = 0 THEN NEW_SLOT = SLOT \ RETURN
4970 NEXT SLOT
4980     PRINT "ERROR " \ MAT PRINT IND, \ STOP
4995                                                         REM

************* Print routine ********************

9000 PRINT
9100    CURRENT_PTR = IND(STORAGE,HEAD)
9200       FOR DA_TA = 1 TO IND(STORAGE,USED)
9300          PRINT IND(CURRENT_PTR,STORED_KEY),
9400          CURRENT_PTR = IND(CURRENT_PTR,NEXT_PTR)
9500       NEXT DA_TA
9550 PRINT \ PRINT
9600    CURRENT_PTR = IND(STORAGE,TAIL)
9700       FOR DA_TA = 1 TO IND(STORAGE,USED)
9800          PRINT IND(CURRENT_PTR,STORED_KEY),
9900          CURRENT_PTR = IND(CURRENT_PTR,REV_PTR)
9950       NEXT DA_TA
10000 END
```

VIII.A.2   Deleting from Linked Lists

One advantage of a two-way linked list, such as the one in the above program, is that it is easy to delete data items from the list.

The following illustrations show the three options and their coding in BASIC.

1. Find the primary key:

```
CURRENT_PTR = IND(STORAGE,HEAD)

FOR FIND_KEY = 1 TO IND(STORAGE,USED)
    IF IND(CURRENT_PTR,STORED_KEY) = PRIMARY_KEY
        THEN RETURN
        ELSE CURRENT_PTR = IND(CURRENT_PTR,NEXT_PTR)
NEXT FIND_KEY
```

2. If the key is the smallest data item in the list, move the key's NEXT_PTR to the HEAD; otherwise, move the key's NEXT_PTR of the row stored in the key's REV_PTR.

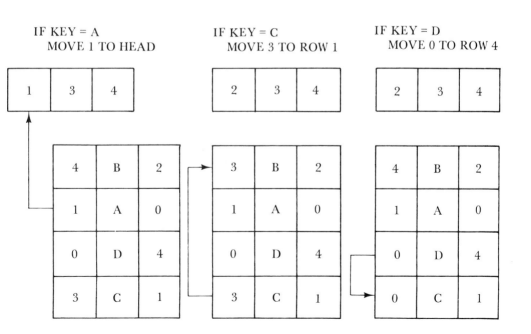

In BASIC:

```
IF CURRENT_PTR = IND (STORAGE, HEAD)                              &
   THEN IND (STORAGE, HEAD) = IND (CURRENT_PTR, NEXT_PTR)      &
   ELSE IND (IND (CURRENT_PTR, NEXT_PTR) , REV_PTR) = IND (CURRENT_PTR, NEXT_PTR)
```

3. If the key is the largest data item in the list, move the
key's NEXT_PTR to the TAIL; otherwise, move the key's
REV_PTR to the key's NEXT_PTR's REV_PTR.

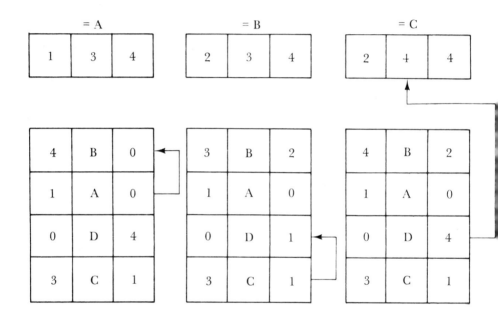

In BASIC:

```
IF CURRENT_PTR = IND (STORAGE, TAIL)                              &
   THEN IND (STORAGE, TAIL) = IND (CURRENT_PTR, REV_PTR)         &
   ELSE IND (IND (CURRENT_PTR, NEXT_PTR) , REV_PTR) = IND (CURRENT_PTR, REV_PTR)
```

4. Then zero the current row and subtract 1 from USED:

= Λ

1	3	3

= B

2	3	3

= C

2	4	3

4	B	0
0	0	0
0	D	4
3	C	1

3	B	2
1	A	0
0	D	1
0	0	0

4	B	2
1	A	0
0	0	0
3	C	1

In BASIC:

```
IND(STORAGE,USED)     =    IND(STORAGE,USED) - 1

IND(CURRENT_PTR,1) = 0
IND(CURRENT_PTR,2) = 0
IND(CURRENT_PTR,3) = 0
```

The arrays in the above examples are small, but imagine a linked list with several hundred data items. Then the changes would indeed be quick and easy: only four statements and the data item has been deleted—but the list is still linked.

VIII.A.3   Sample Program

The following program will create and maintain a two-way linked list—with all the options. It is not meant to be a model program. Each line of code is therefore not as compact as possible. It is designed to give an overview to and guidance for anyone wishing to construct such a list for their own purposes.

Again, the best way to study this program is to create your own arrays on paper. Then spend some time walking through each step. Time spent on this program will provide the necessary background for a course in data base processing. It will be worth the effort.

```
**************** set values for variables ********

50 DECLARE INTEGER PRIMARY_KEY, PREVIOUS_PTR, NEXT_PTR, STORED_KEY        &
                , STORAGE, HEAD, SIZE, USED, REV_PTR
100 NEXT_PTR = 1 \ STORED_KEY = 2 \ STORAGE = 0 \ HEAD = 1 \ TAIL = 2
110 USED = 3 \ REV_PTR = 3
150                                                        REM
200 DIM IND(6,3) \ SIZE = 6
250                                                        REM

    ************* menu *******************************

500 PRINT "  Choose option:  1- list ascending      2- list descending "
510 PRINT "                  3- modify record(s)  4- add record(s)      "
520 PRINT "                  5- delete record(s)  6- end session        "
530 INPUT "   Option ==> "; OPTION%
540 IF OPTION% = 0 THEN 500
570 ON OPTION% GOTO 1000, 2000, 3000, 4000, 5000, 10000
595                                                        REM

    ************** print lists **********************

1000 PRINT \ GOSUB 9000
1100         GOTO 500
2000 PRINT \ GOSUB 9550
2010         GOTO 500

    ************** module can be added to update contents ***

3000 PRINT \ PRINT "NOT READY" \ GOTO 500
3095                                                       REM
```

```
          ************* 4000 = add records *******************

4000 IF IND(STORAGE,HEAD) = 0 THEN 4100                    &
         ELSE IF IND(STORAGE,USED) = SIZE THEN             &
         PRINT "Index Full" \ GOTO 500
4010                                                                REM
4100 PRINT \ INPUT "Enter primary key (0) ==> "; PRIMARY_KEY
4150 PRINT
4200       IF PRIMARY_KEY = 0 THEN PRINT          \ &
              PRINT IND(0,1), IND(0,2), IND(0,3) \ PRINT \ &
              MAT PRINT IND, \ GOTO 500
4250 IF IND(STORAGE,HEAD) = 0 THEN 4750
4300 CURRENT_PTR = IND(STORAGE,HEAD) \ PREVIOUS_PTR = CURRENT_PTR
4400 FOR KEY_SEARCH = 1 TO IND(STORAGE,USED)
4410     IF PRIMARY_KEY < IND(CURRENT_PTR,STORED_KEY) THEN 4630
4420     IF PRIMARY_KEY = IND(CURRENT_PTR,STORED_KEY)                &
                          THEN PRINT "DUPLICATE KEY " \  GOTO 4100
4430     PREVIOUS_PTR = CURRENT_PTR
4440     CURRENT_PTR  = IND(CURRENT_PTR,NEXT_PTR)
4450 NEXT KEY_SEARCH
4490                                                                REM
4540 GOSUB 4950
4550       IND(NEW_SLOT,STORED_KEY) = PRIMARY_KEY
4560       IND(NEW_SLOT,NEXT_PTR)   = 0
4570       IND(PREVIOUS_PTR,NEXT_PTR) = NEW_SLOT
4572       IND(NEW_SLOT,REV_PTR) = IND(STORAGE,TAIL)
4576       IND(STORAGE,TAIL) = NEW_SLOT
4580       IND(STORAGE,USED) = IND(STORAGE,USED) + 1
4590 REM PRINT IND(0,1), IND(0,2), IND(0,3) \ REM PRINT
4592 REM MAT PRINT IND, \ PRINT \ GOTO 4100
4593 GOTO 4000
4595                                                                REM
4630 GOSUB 4950
4640       IND(NEW_SLOT,STORED_KEY) = PRIMARY_KEY
4650       IND(NEW_SLOT,NEXT_PTR)   = CURRENT_PTR
4670       IND(STORAGE,USED) = IND(STORAGE,USED) + 1
4680       IF PRIMARY_KEY < IND(IND(STORAGE,HEAD), STORED_KEY)      &
              THEN IND(STORAGE,HEAD) = NEW_SLOT \                   &
                   IND(PREVIOUS_PTR,REV_PTR) = NEW_SLOT \           &
                   IND(NEW_SLOT,REV_PTR) = 0                        &
              ELSE IND(PREVIOUS_PTR,NEXT_PTR) = NEW_SLOT    \       &
                   IND(NEW_SLOT,REV_PTR) = IND(CURRENT_PTR,REV_PTR) \ &
                   IND(CURRENT_PTR,REV_PTR) = NEW_SLOT
4690 REM PRINT IND(0,1), IND(0,2), IND(0,3) \ REM PRINT
4692 REM MAT PRINT IND, \ GOTO 4100
4693 GOTO 4000
4695                                                                REM
4750       IND(1,STORED_KEY) = PRIMARY_KEY
4760       IND(1,NEXT_PTR)   = 0
4780       IND(STORAGE,HEAD) = 1
4782       IND(CURRENT_PTR,REV_PTR) = 0
4786       IND(STORAGE,TAIL)  = 1
4788       IND(STORAGE,USED)  = IND(STORAGE,USED) + 1
4790 REM PRINT IND(0,1), IND(0,2), IND(0,3) \ REM PRINT
4792 REM MAT PRINT IND, \ PRINT \ GOTO 4100
4793 GOTO 4000
4795                                                                REM
4950 FOR SLOT = 1 TO SIZE
4960       IF IND(SLOT,STORED_KEY) = 0 THEN NEW_SLOT = SLOT \ RETURN
4970 NEXT SLOT
4980       PRINT "ERROR " \ MAT PRINT IND, \ STOP
4995                                                                REM
```

```
************* 5000 = delete records ******************

5000 PRINT \ INPUT "Enter primary key (0) ==> "; PRIMARY_KEY
5010 PRINT \ IF PRIMARY_KEY = 0 THEN 500
5100 GOSUB 5900
5110    IF CURRENT_PTR = 0 THEN 500
5200 IF CURRENT_PTR = IND(STORAGE, HEAD)                              &
        THEN IND(STORAGE, HEAD) = IND(CURRENT_PTR, NEXT_PTR)         &
        ELSE IND(IND(CURRENT_PTR, REV_PTR), NEXT_PTR) = IND(CURRENT_PTR, NEXT_PTR
5300 IF CURRENT_PTR = IND(STORAGE, TAIL)                             &
        THEN IND(STORAGE, TAIL) = IND(CURRENT_PTR, REV_PTR)         &
        ELSE IND(IND(CURRENT_PTR, NEXT_PTR), REV_PTR) = IND(CURRENT_PTR, REV_PTR)
5400 IND(STORAGE, USED) = IND(STORAGE, USED) - 1
5500 IND(CURRENT_PTR, 1) = 0 \ IND(CURRENT_PTR, 2) = 0 \ IND(CURRENT_PTR, 3) = 0
5600 PRINT IND(0, 1), IND(0, 2), IND(0, 3) \ PRINT
5610 MAT PRINT IND, \ PRINT
5700 GOTO 5000
5900                                                        REM
5910 IF IND(STORAGE, HEAD) = 0 THEN 5960 ELSE CURRENT_PTR = IND(STORAGE, HEAD)
5920 FOR FIND_KEY = 1 TO IND(STORAGE, USED)
5930    IF IND(CURRENT_PTR, STORED_KEY) = PRIMARY_KEY&
           THEN RETURN
5940      CURRENT_PTR = IND(CURRENT_PTR, NEXT_PTR)
5950 NEXT FIND_KEY
5960 PRINT "KEY does not exist" \ CURRENT_PTR = 0 \ RETURN
5995                                                        REM

************* 9000 = print routines ******************

9000 PRINT
9100    CURRENT_PTR = IND(STORAGE, HEAD)
9200       FOR DA_TA = 1 TO IND(STORAGE, USED)
9300          PRINT IND(CURRENT_PTR, STORED_KEY),
9400          CURRENT_PTR = IND(CURRENT_PTR, NEXT_PTR)
9500       NEXT DA_TA
9510 PRINT
9525 RETURN
9550 PRINT \ PRINT
9600    CURRENT_PTR = IND(STORAGE, TAIL)
9700       FOR DA_TA = 1 TO IND(STORAGE, USED)
9800          PRINT IND(CURRENT_PTR, STORED_KEY),
9900          CURRENT_PTR = IND(CURRENT_PTR, REV_PTR)
9950       NEXT DA_TA
9953 PRINT
9955 RETURN
10000 END
```

VIII.B   REVIEW QUESTIONS

1. In your own words, explain how a linked list works.

2. What is a single linked list? A multiple linked list?

3. How are the following used in the sample programs:

    a. HEAD
    b. CURRENT_PTR
    c. PREVIOUS_PTR
    d. REV_PTR
    e. STORED_KEY
    f. NEXT_PTR
    g. STORAGE
    h. USED

4. When adding or deleting from linked lists, what are the main considerations and possible error conditions?

5. How are linked lists stored in programs? How are they stored between runs?

6. List some of the advantages and disadvantages of using linked lists. How might linked lists be used in developing systems software?

VIII.C EXERCISES

1. Using pencil and paper, draw an array (6,3) and insert the keys "5", "1", "3", and "6" respectively. Then add forward and reverse pointers.

2. Into the above array, insert the key "2". Be sure to change the relevant pointers.

3. Then delete the key "5", changing all relevant pointers.

4. Using the sample program for multiple linked lists, chart and write a program to maintain a linked list of student I.D. numbers. Design the program carefully, developing and testing one module at a time.

5. Finish the module from line 3000 of the sample program at the end of the chapter by adding a relative file with enough records for each of the student I.D.s in Exercise 4. Add subroutines so that data for each student can be maintained in the relative file. Each relative key to the file is to be stored in the fourth column of the linked list.

Forward		Reverse	File Key
—	787634	—	
—	243761	—	2
—	185892	—	

Cell 2

(Remember to add routines to store the arrays between runs.)

IX
Inverted Lists

IX.A INVERTED LISTS

The linked lists discussed in the previous chapter provide a method for handling primary keys. The keys in the lists can be combined with disk addresses, relative keys, etc., to indicate the exact storage location of data items or of records. It is, however, often useful to know which of the primary keys can be associated with a value stored in another field within the same record. We might ask how many blue, king-size sheets are in stock, or how much 2" black plastic pipe is in the warehouse. In such cases, the primay key, or stock number, can be used to locate records, but there remains the need for a method to examine the contents of the record. We need a method for asking questions about our data.

The questions themselves are termed *queries*, and the files containing the needed values *query files*. A query is a request for a subset of records that have one common denominator, for example, blue, plastic, etc. A list of those records that share a single attribute is called an *inverted list*. For the two questions above, if the query file contained only sheets, then we would need an inverted file for color and one for size. For the plastic pipe, we might need files for length and for color.

The values stored in inverted files are often simply called *secondary keys*. In most computer languages, they are defined somewhere in the record definition statements. Secondary keys usually have duplicate values, and these values can be changed. It is worthwhile, however, to remember that *as values are changed, the inverted list for these values must also be changed*. Otherwise, queries will receive incorrect responses.

The array on page 169 contains an inventory table. It represents the query file. Each row might also be considered a record in a relative file. The two inverted files are created to answer the question "What is the total length of 2" black plastic pipe on hand?"

The arrays SIZE and COLOR on page 170 represent inverted lists. The numbers stored in the array cells refer to row numbers in the query file. SIZE(1,1) contains the row number of part 126701, SIZE(1,2) the row for part 126901, SIZE(1,3) the row for part 127701, and SIZE(1,4) the row for part 127901. These are all part numbers for pipes with 1" diameter.

Instead of row numbers, primary keys might have been stored in the inverted lists. In smaller sets, it is usually faster to store and reference row numbers. This is, of course, not always possible, but when primary keys are used, more overhead is needed to search the linked lists.

In either case, the row numbers or the primary keys will automatically be stored in ascending order in an inverted list. This helps hold down overhead and means the inverted list can be processed sequentially.

In BASIC, the two lists can be matched to answer our question: "What is the total length 2" black plastic pipe on hand?"

```
FOR SIZE = 1 TO 10
  FOR COLOR = 1 TO 10
    IF SIZE = COLOR THEN &
      TOTAL = TOTAL + INV(SIZE, INV(SIZE, 3)) * INV(SIZE, (INV(SIZE, 5))
    NEXT COLOR
NEXT SIZE

PRINT "AMOUNT OF 2" BLACK PLASTIC PIPE = "; TOTAL
```

DIM INV(16, 5) The query file.

	PART NO	SIZE	LENGTH	COLOR	ON-HAND
(1)	126701	1	8	BLACK	10
(2)	126801	2	8	BLACK	27
(3)	126804	3	8	BLACK	18
(4)	126808	4	8	BLACK	12
(5)	126901	1	12	BLACK	10
(6)	126904	2	12	BLACK	8
(7)	126910	3	12	BLACK	12
(8)	126915	4	12	BLACK	14
(9)	127701	1	8	WHITE	7
(10)	127801	2	8	WHITE	16
(11)	127802	3	8	WHITE	12
(12)	127804	4	8	WHITE	21
(13)	127901	1	12	WHITE	0
(14)	127910	2	12	WHITE	4
(15)	127912	3	12	WHITE	16
(16)	127916	4	12	WHITE	12

PRIMARY   SECONDARY   SECONDARY
  KEY   KEY   KEY

The result would be matches between the values in row 2 and in row 6 of the query file, as shown on page 170.

Several points should be remembered about inverted files.

First, secondary keys impose a structure on data files. Otherwise, these files remain simply a (linked) list of data records.

Second, secondary keys define relations between items in data records. They are similar to a book's index in that they enable a

DIM SIZE(4, 10)   Inverted file for pipe size.

1″	1	5	9	13						
2″	2	6	10	14						
3″	3	7	11	15						
4″	4	8	12	16						

DIM COLOR(2, 10)   Inverted file for pipe color.

BLACK	1	2	3	4	5	6	7	8		
WHITE	9	10	11	12	13	14	15	16		

SIZE

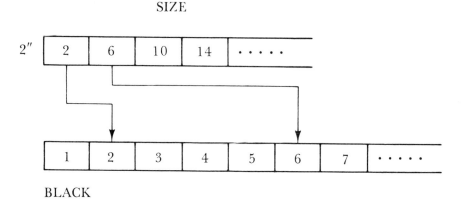

BLACK

COLOR

more detailed examination of its contents than the actual Table of Contents.

And third, they are tools for creating information systems. Inverted lists and secondary keys establish relationships among data items that are not always apparent when the data items are entered into the system.

IX.A.1   Overflow Tables

Inverted lists are usually built when needed because each time the value of a secondary key field is changed, any previous tables are no longer valid. The actual size of array for a particular list cannot, therefore, always be known when the program is written. To solve this problem, *overflow tables* are created. They contain a pointer at the end of each full row. The pointer indicates which row is the next logical row in the list. Thus, if a subset of a data item contains more values than can be fit into one row, these values are simply continued in another row. The pointer at the end of the first row indicates the location of the "overflow" row.

In the following example, pipe sizes and their row locations are stored in an overflow table. The first row of the table begins with the pipe size (= 1") and the row location for 1" pipe (= row 2). Rows 1 and 2 are now used: row 1 for the above information and row 2 for the row locations in the query (INV) table. The next unused row is then row 3.

DIM SIZE(8, 5)

	Inches	Row Location			
(1)	1	2			
(2)	1				
(3)					

Unused = 3

SIZE(1,1) contains the pipe size 1"; and SIZE(1,2) contains a pointer to row 2 where references to the query (INV) table will be stored. SIZE(2,1) indicates that information on 1" pipe can be found in row 1 of the inventory table.

The next item in the inventory table is a 2" pipe. This is entered in the first row, along with a pointer to the row where information for 2" pipe will be stored.

	Inches	Row Location			
(1)	1	2	2	3	
(2)	1				
(3)	2				
(4)					

Unused = 4

Because there is no longer room in the first row for an entry for 3" pipe, a pointer is entered in column 5 indicating the overflow row.

					Overflow
(1)	1	2	2	3	4
(2)	1				
(3)	2				
(4)	3	5			
(5)	3				

Unused = 6

SI_ZE(4,1) contains the size for 3" pipe, and SI_ZE(4,2) the location of the row (5) where a pointer to a row in the query table (INV) can be found.

If we were to use primary keys instead of row pointers, a full inverted file for the INV tables would be as follows.

1	2	2	3	4
126701	126901	127701	127901	
126801	126904	127801	127910	
3	5	4	6	
126804	126910	127802	127912	
126808	126915	127804	127916	

Unused = 7   Overflow

An inverted file for COLOR can be constructed by assigning numerical values to each color: BLACK = 1 and WHITE = 2. Note the use of the overflow column to continue the list of primary keys.

1	2	2	4	
126701	126801	126804	126808	3
126901	126904	126910	126915	
127701	127801	127802	127804	5
127901	127910	127912	127916	

Unused = 6   Overflow

IX.A.2   Searching Inverted Lists

Inverted lists are searched in the same manner in which they are created. Cells containing secondary keys are examined until a match is found. Overflow pointers are followed when a row does not contain the needed key. Once a match is found, the next cell contains a pointer to the row containing the primary keys (or the location of the primary keys in the query file).

```
 10 PTR_ROW = 1 \ OVERFLOW = 5

100 FOR CELL = 1 TO 4 STEP 2

110    IF SI_ZE (PTR_ROW, CELL) = SIZE_KEY THEN 200
120 NEXT CELL
130 PTR_ROW = SI_ZE (PTR_ROW, OVERFLOW)
140 GOTO 100

200 DATA_ROW = SI_ZE (PTR_ROW, (CELL + 1))

300 FOR CELL = 1 TO 4

      [ match using: SI_ZE (DATA_ROW, CELL) ]

350 NEXT CELL
360 DATA_ROW = SI_ZE (DATA_ROW, OVERFLOW)
370 GOTO 300
```

IX.B   SUMMARY

The last three chapters introduced indexed sequential files, using primary and secondary keys. This type of file organization is extremely important for the construction of data systems. Because of the nature of introducing programming skills and because of the limited amount of time available, indexed sequential files are quite often not taught to the student. This can continue for a series of introductory level courses in various computer languages. But a mastery of indexed sequential files is necessary before more advanced data systems can be designed and put into operation. Continued use of sequential files, without recourse to advanced file organizations, would indeed prove limiting.

The chapters on linked lists and inverted lists demonstrate the programming of primary and secondary keys. Once these basic concepts are understood, it is easier to use many of the record management and data base systems on the market. It is, of course, less a matter of programming skills than of logic and data management. Good data management depends upon understanding and programming the relations among data items. Linked and inverted lists are basic tools.

IX.C SAMPLE PROGRAM

This program builds two arrays—one (IND) to hold a linked list for the PRIMARY_KEY, and a second (SI_ZE) to hold an inverted file for the SIZE_KEY (the pipe diameter).

Since the linked list is taken from the previous chapter, only the inverted list needs study in detail. It begins at line 5000, and is referenced from lines 4580, 4685, and 4790 as a subroutine.

NOTE: In this example, arrays can overflow if too may data items are entered = subscript out of range. This is done to limit the lines of code.

```
50 DECLARE INTEGER PRIMARY_KEY, PREVIOUS_PTR, NEXT_PTR, STORED_KEY          &
              , STORAGE, HEAD, SIZE, USED, FIND_SLOT
75 DECLARE INTEGER SIZE_KEY, COLOR_KEY, OVERFLOW, UNUSED, EMPTY
85 DECLARE INTEGER PTR_ROW, DATA_ROW
100 NEXT_PTR = 1 \ STORED_KEY = 2 \ STORAGE = 0 \ HEAD = 1 \ SIZE = 2
110 USED = 3 \ UNUSED = 1 \ OVERFLOW = 5 \ EMPTY = 0
150                                                      REM
200 DIM IND(15,3) \ IND(STORAGE,SIZE) = 15
210 DIM SI_ZE(10,5) \ SI_ZE(STORAGE,SIZE) = 10 \ SI_ZE(STORAGE,UNUSED) = 2
```

```
**********************************************************
*                                                        *
*                         MENU                           *
*                                                        *
* Obtain primary key and pipe diameter.   0 for          *
* key can be used to stop the program and examine        *
* the contents of the arrays.                            *
*                                                        *
**********************************************************

4000 IF IND(STORAGE,HEAD) = 0 THEN 4100                              &
         ELSE IF IND(STORAGE,SIZE) = IND(STORAGE,USED) THEN          &
            PRINT "Index Full" \ GOTO 9000
4010                                                          REM
4100 INPUT "Enter primary key   (0) ==> "; PRIMARY_KEY
4200      IF PRIMARY_KEY = 0 THEN 9000
4210 INPUT "Enter Pipe Diameter     ==> "; SIZE_KEY
4220   IF SIZE_KEY > 4 THEN PRINT "Illegal size" \ GOTO 4210
```

```
*****************************************************
*                                                   *
*   Lines 4250 - 4995 build the linked list for     *
*                 the primary key                   *
*                                                   *
*   4580, 4685, and 4790 GOSUB for the inverted     *
*                     list                          *
*                                                   *
*****************************************************
```

```
4250 IF IND(STORAGE,HEAD) = 0 THEN 4750
4300 CURRENT_PTR = IND(STORAGE,HEAD) \ PREVIOUS_PTR = CURRENT_PTR
4400 FOR KEY_SEARCH = 1 TO IND(STORAGE,USED)
4410     IF PRIMARY_KEY < IND(CURRENT_PTR,STORED_KEY) THEN 4630
4420     IF PRIMARY_KEY = IND(CURRENT_PTR, STORED_KEY)                       &
                      THEN PRINT "DUPLICATE KEY " \ GOTO 4100
4430     PREVIOUS_PTR = CURRENT_PTR
4440     CURRENT_PTR = IND(CURRENT_PTR,NEXT_PTR)
4450 NEXT KEY_SEARCH
4490                                                     REM
4540 GOSUB 4950
4550     IND(NEW_SLOT,STORED_KEY) = PRIMARY_KEY
4560     IND(NEW_SLOT,NEXT_PTR)   = 0
4570     IND(PREVIOUS_PTR,NEXT_PTR) = NEW_SLOT
4575     IND(STORAGE,USED)   = IND(STORAGE,USED) + 1
4580 GOSUB 5000
4590 GOTO 4100
4595                                                     REM
4630 GOSUB 4950
4640     IND(NEW_SLOT,STORED_KEY) = PRIMARY_KEY
4650     IND(NEW_SLOT,NEXT_PTR)   = CURRENT_PTR
4670     IND(STORAGE,USED) = IND(STORAGE,USED) + 1
4680     IF PRIMARY_KEY < IND(IND(STORAGE,HEAD), STORED_KEY)                 &
                  THEN IND(STORAGE,HEAD) = NEW_SLOT                          &
                  ELSE IND(PREVIOUS_PTR,NEXT_PTR) = NEW_SLOT
4685 GOSUB 5000
4690 GOTO 4100
4695                                                     REM
4750     IND(1,STORED_KEY) = PRIMARY_KEY
4760     IND(1,NEXT_PTR)   = 0
4780     IND(STORAGE,HEAD)   = 1
4785     IND(STORAGE,USED)   = IND(STORAGE,USED) + 1
4790 GOSUB 5000
4793 GOTO 4100
4795                                                     REM
4950 FOR SLOT = 1 TO IND(STORAGE,SIZE)
4955     IF IND(STORAGE,SIZE) = IND(STORAGE,USED) THEN                       &
              PRINT "Index Full" \ GOTO 4100
4960     IF IND(SLOT,STORED_KEY) = 0 THEN NEW_SLOT = SLOT \ RETURN
4970 NEXT SLOT
4980     PRINT "ERROR " \ MAT PRINT IND, \ STOP
4995                                                     REM
```

```
**********************************************
*                                            *
*              INVERTED LIST                 *
*                                            *
*    5100-5250 LOCATE row to store keys      *
*                                            *
*          5110 = key already exists         *
*          5120 = new key, enter row         *
*          5200 = set-up overflow            *
*                                            *
**********************************************

5000 IF SI__ZE (STORAGE, UNUSED) > SI__ZE (STORAGE, SIZE)                     &
          THEN PRINT "Size Table Full" \ MAT PRINT SI__ZE, \ STOP
5020 PTR__ROW = 1
5030                                                              REM
5100 FOR CELL = 1 TO 4 STEP 2
5110    IF SI__ZE (PTR__ROW, CELL) = SIZE__KEY THEN 5500
5120    IF SI__ZE (PTR__ROW, CELL) = EMPTY THEN                               &
             SI__ZE (PTR__ROW, CELL) = SIZE__KEY                    \         &
             SI__ZE (PTR__ROW, (CELL + 1)) = SI__ZE (STORAGE, UNUSED) \       &
             SI__ZE (STORAGE, UNUSED) = SI__ZE (STORAGE, UNUSED) + 1 \        &
             GOTO 5500
5130 NEXT CELL
5140                                                              REM
5200 IF SI__ZE (PTR__ROW, OVERFLOW) <> EMPTY THEN 5210                        &
        ELSE SI__ZE (PTR__ROW, OVERFLOW) = SI__ZE (STORAGE, UNUSED)  \        &
             SI__ZE (STORAGE, UNUSED) = SI__ZE (STORAGE, UNUSED) + 1
5210 PTR__ROW = SI__ZE (PTR__ROW, OVERFLOW)
5220 GOTO 5100
5250                                                              REM

     **********************************************
     *                                            *
     *    5500-5590 ENTER key into array          *
     *                                            *
     *          5520 = space available, enter key *
     *          5550 = set-up overflow            *
     *                                            *
     **********************************************

5500 DATA__ROW = SI__ZE (PTR__ROW, (CELL + 1))
5505                                                              REM
5510 FOR CELL = 1 TO 4
5520    IF SI__ZE (DATA__ROW, CELL) = EMPTY                              &
          THEN SI__ZE (DATA__ROW, CELL) = PRIMARY__KEY \ RETURN
5530 NEXT CELL
5540                                                              REM
5550 IF SI__ZE (DATA__ROW, OVERFLOW) <> EMPTY THEN 5560                  &
        ELSE SI__ZE (DATA__ROW, OVERFLOW) = SI__ZE (STORAGE, UNUSED)  \ &
             SI__ZE (STORAGE, UNUSED) = SI__ZE (STORAGE, UNUSED) + 1
5560 DATA__ROW = SI__ZE (DATA__ROW, OVERFLOW)
5570 GOTO 5510
5580 PRINT "ERROR" \ MAT PRINT SI__ZE, \ STOP
5590                                                              REM
```

```
**************************************************
*                                                *
*                PRINT ROUTINES                  *
*                                                *
**************************************************

9000 PRINT
9050 PRINT "PRIMARY TABLE" \ PRINT
9100    CURRENT_PTR = IND (STORAGE, HEAD)
9200       FOR DA_TA = 1 TO IND (STORAGE, USED)
9300          PRINT IND (CURRENT_PTR, STORED_KEY) ,
9400          CURRENT_PTR = IND (CURRENT_PTR, NEXT_PTR)
9500       NEXT DA_TA
9600 PRINT \ PRINT
9700                                                          REM
9710 PRINT \ PRINT "PRIMARY INDEX" \ PRINT                          \ &
     PRINT IND (0, 1) , IND (0, 2) , IND (0, 3) \ MAT PRINT IND,     \ &
     PRINT \ PRINT "SIZE INDEX" \ PRINT                             \ &
     PRINT SI_ZE (0, 1) , SI_ZE (0, 2) , SI_ZE (0, 3) \ MAT PRINT SI_ZE,

9720 INPUT "STOP (Y/N) ==> "; ANS$ \ IF ANS$ = "N" THEN 4100
9999 END
```

IX.D REVIEW QUESTIONS

1. What are inverted files and why are they constructed? For what types of applications could they be used?

2. Explain the relationship between values stored in an inverted list and the same values stored in records. Of what value is an inverted list if one of the corresponding values in just one of the records is changed?

3. Why is it necessary to carefully consider which data items will be used as secondary keys? Why is system overhead greater for secondary keys than for primary keys?

4. Using the example in this chapter of a query for the relation between SIZE and COLOR, explain how inverted lists are matched to obtain the correct response to a query.

5. Can a distinction be made between data and information? In this chapter, which might be which?

6. Explain how an overflow table works. Why are such tables created? Explain lines 5100–5210 and 5510–5570 of the sample program.

7. Why is there no section in this chapter on deleting from inverted files?

IX.E EXERCISES

1. Using the query file (INV) at the beginning of this chapter, draw and complete an inverted list for 'LENGTH'.

2. Draw a diagram similar to the one matching SIZE and COLOR to demonstrate how the query "How much 2" X 8' pipe is on hand?" would be answered.

3. Using the sample program, add an array COLOR and write a subroutine to build an inverted list to hold the primary keys for WHITE and BLACK pipe. The flowcharts after lines 5250 and 5590 can be used as guides.

4. Again using the sample program, diagram, write, and test a subroutine to answer queries similar to the one used in this chapter "How much 2" black plastic pipe is on hand?" Be sure to use handdrawn arrays and carefully test all charts and diagrams before writing the program. Also, consider carefully how the user is to enter queries and receive responses. It will also be necessary to limit searches to the size of the arrays or subscript errors will occur.

X
BLOCK I/O

X.A BLOCK I/O VS. MAGNETIC TAPE
AND RELATIVE FILES

BLOCK I/O is very similar in concept to the blocking routines used in moving data to and from magnetic tape. Records are assembled in an I/O buffer until some upper limit is reached. They are then stored and retrieved as a unit—or block of data. In the case of magnetic tape, the upper limit is prescribed by the capabilities of internal storage and the tape drive.

The storage medium for BLOCK I/O is disk. The upper limit is usually assumed to be the number of bytes of storage per disk sector. Most systems are formatted to accept 512 bytes per sector.

The similarity to relative files is found in the manner in which sectors are used to store blocks of data. Each sector can be compared to a relative cell. But where each relative cell holds an individual record, BLOCK I/O writes groups of records to a single cell—or sector.

180

One Record

			. . . .

Relative File

Several Records

			. . . .

Disk Sector

Blocking and deblocking of the records in the I/O buffer is under control of the program.

In theory, reading and writing a sector of data, rather than a record of data, provides for better utilization of disk space and faster overall processing times. And this is true. Because records can be blocked to better fill a sector, less space remains unused at the end of the sector, and because less system interrupts occur when groups of records are read than when single records are read, processing times are faster. Wasted space and unnecessary interrupts increase system costs.

This is why modern disk systems automatically and routinely block and deblock records. If nothing else, it is a form of self defense. To remain competitive, computer vendors must design products that offer the greatest efficiency and possible return on investment. But there is more to it than this.

X.B   BLOCK I/O AND INDEXED LISTS

Since modern systems block records automatically, applications programmers tend not to concern themselves with managing disk space. Not too long ago, it was necessary to count bytes, plan sector utilization, and allocate cylinders. There was a real danger that an application would overflow its allocated space and ABORT. This danger is usually no longer of serious concern. The system will find space somewhere as long as the disk is not completly full.

Nonetheless, a lack of concern for disk utilization can become expensive. When compiled programs have to be unnecessarily paged because allocated work space is too small, time is wasted. When a read–write head on a disk has to move continuously back and forth because data is stored all over the place, time is wasted.

When large lists or arrays are broken into subsets for storage, and searches are made through each subset until a data item is found, time is wasted. And when an application processes several hundred thousand transactions each run, wasted time accumulates quickly. It can mean an inefficient operation—not to mention overtime, another shift, or simply less processing time to market.

BLOCK I/O is one of the tools available to programmers for steamlining applications. There are times when programmers want to know exactly which and how much data is stored in an I/O bufer or on a disk sector. For example, if one has a very large linked list—stock numbers, etc.—it is sometimes best to read and search only the sector containing the needed data.

This can be accomplished by letting the first sector contain an array of pointers to other sectors, and they in turn contain subsets of the linked list.

Block 1		Block 2	Block 3
10	2	1	11
20	3	2	12
30	4	3	13
40	5	4	14
50	6	5	15
60	7	6	16
70	8	7	17
		8	18
		9	19
		10	20

Pointers   Subset 1   Subset 2

BLOCK 1 contains pointers to subsets of stock numbers. If the stock number is 10 or less, then the data will be in block 2. If the number is greater than 10, but 20 or less, then the data will be in block 3, etc. (Since these numbers are consecutive, a little math would locate the relative block—but stock numbers are rarely consecutive.) The first block is stored in an array in memory and used to read (or call) other blocks as needed.

It is also possible for blocks to reference blocks, which in turn reference other blocks.

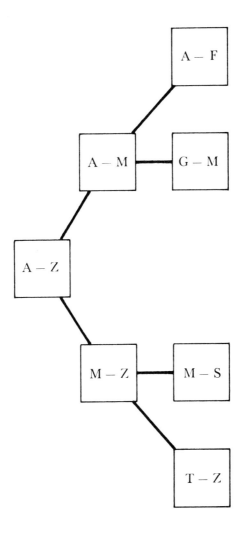

This method can be used for both linked and inverted lists, as well as for larger arrays amd tables.

On smaller and medium-sized computers, blocked records can accomplish a lot a work quickly and efficiently. The trick is to carefully consider the application, the data, and the user before programming. Almost anyone can write a program. Good applications programmers design and code programs that make the best utilization of the system—while serving the user's actual needs.

X.C   BLOCK I/O PROCESSING

The approach to BLOCK I/O files is basically the same as for programming relative records. One might call BLOCK I/O "relative sector" processing. Each relative file cell contains one record of data. Each BLOCK I/O cell contains one or more records, with the program specifying the location of the record in the cell. The closer the total number of bytes for all the records in the cell is to 512 (or the number of bytes per sector), the less wasted or blank space at the end of the sector.

X.C.1   Creating BLOCK I/O Files: OPEN

BLOCK I/O is a logical breakdown of physical storage space. The storage space itself is the disk sector, and the I/O buffers are in turn equal in size to the number of bytes per sector.

One sector = 512 = I/O buffer size

Rec 1	Rec 2	Rec 3	Rec 4	Rec 5	12 spaces
100 bytes	100 bytes	100 bytes	100 bytes	100 bytes	12 bytes

The file containing the blocked records is OPENed for INPUT or OUTPUT, with ORGANIZATION VIRTUAL.

```
ln OPEN file FOR INPUT AS FILE #n       &
        , ORGANIZATION VIRTUAL

100 OPEN 'MASTER.DAT' FOR OUTPUT AS FILE #1      &
        , ORGANIZATION VIRTUAL
```

Record size will be 512 bytes, or a multiple as close to 512 as possible. The programmer then blocks and deblocks the records.

X.C.2   Writing BLOCK I/O: PUT

PUT is used to write a block of data to the disk sector. The format is basically the same as for relative records, except that it is now relative blocks.

    A. ln PUT #n

    B. ln PUT #n, RECORD n

In this context, "RECORD n" indicates a relative block position!

PUT is used to move blocks of data from the buffer to the disk. Each PUT writes a block, beginning with the beginning of a sector.

Example A is used to write blocks sequentially. Sequential PUTs create logical sequential blocks.

Example B specifies the exact cell of the file where the block of data is to be stored.

NOTE: PUT overwrites data!

When PUT is used to move data, the system does not check to see if data already exists on the sector. No error message will be returned.

NOTE ALSO: "RECORD n" can move more than one record!

400 PUT #1, RECORD 10%

would actually move the contents of the buffer to logical sector 10. As in the example above, if the buffer held five records, then five records would be moved to the logical sector.

X.C.3 Retrieving Blocks: GET

GET retrieves stored blocks, or sectors of data. Sequential GETs retrieve blocks sequentially, and random GETs, when used with a record number, retrieve data from individual sectors.

A. ln GET #n
B. ln GET #n, RECORD n

NOTE:

400 GET #1, RECORD 10%

will not retrieve the 10th record, but the 10th logical block of records.

Because of the nature of BLOCK I/O files, records are not deleted or updated by specific commands. To delete a record, remove any reference to its location. To update a record, GET the block, change the contents of the records, and PUT the block back in its original place.

X.C.4   Special Considerations: FILL

FILL items are null characters. They are not written when data is moved to a storage location. Yet they mask, or skip over, portions of the I/O buffer.   One might say that FILL items are used to ignore for a current operation some portion or portions of internal storage. When blocks of data are created using FILL, the result is space(s). When processing blocks, FILL skips over data.

MAP (EXAMPLE)	FIRST_NAME$	=	20%	&
	FILL$	=	2%	&
	MIDDLE_INIT$	=	2%	&
	FILL$	=	2%	&
	LAST_NAME$	=	20%	
MAP (EXAMPLE)	DATA_REC%	=	46%	

In the above example, spaces are reserved between data items. DATA_REC$ can, therefore, be printed or displayed without further programming. The spacing is contained within the MAP.
Normally, the default values for FILL are:

Real:	FILL	=	4 bytes
Integer:	FILL%	=	2 bytes
String:	FILL$	=	16 bytes

or, as in the MAP above, size can be determined by the program:

$$FILL\$ = 2\%$$

X.C.5   (DE)Blocking: MOVE

As with relative records, I/O buffers are either statically or dynamically defined. When using BLOCK I/O, however, the advantage is normally with dynamic routines. MAP statements can be used to some advantage when record sizes are large and only a limited number of data items are stored within each block.
MOVE TO and MOVE FROM are used to transfer data from one work area to another within internal memory. MOVE does not read or write data. This is done with PUT and GET.

X.C.5.a   Static

Assume one wanted to transfer a large deck of computer punch cards to disk. An additional 80 characters are to be reserved at the end of each record. One might use several MAP statements, and then PUT the data to disk.

```
MAP (NEW) CARD1$ = 80%, FILL$ = 432%
MAP (NEW) FILL$ = 160%, CARD2$ = 80%, FILL$ = 272%
MAP (NEW) FILL$ = 320%, CARD3$ = 80%, FILL$ = 112%

INPUT CARD1$
INPUT CARD2$
INPUT CARD3$

PUT #n
```

This example is a fast method for copying and reformatting data. It is, of course, greatly simplified and limited in application. MAP statements are considered static and cannot be further defined or increased once the program is compiled.

S.C.5.b Dynamic

A more workable application for BLOCK I/O is illustrated by the following example. The data is to be entered through a CRT and stored on disk.

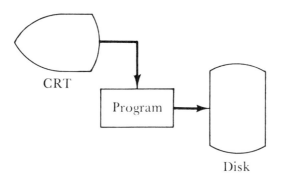

Record layout:	NAME	A	30
	ADDRESS	A	30
	CITY	A	16
	STATE	A	2
	ZIP	N	5

In BASIC:

```
10 FOR X = 0 TO 5         ! 6 records as a unit
      INPUT "NAME (0 = STOP)      = => "; NAME$
        IF NAME$ = "0" THEN 100
      INPUT "ADDRESS               = => "; ADDRESS$
      INPUT "CITY                  = => "; CITY$
      INPUT "ZIP                   = => "; ZIP%

50    MOVE TO #1, FILL$ = X * 80, NAME$ = 30%                    &
                  , ADDRESS$ = 30%, CITY$ = 2%, ZIP%

60 NEXT X

70 PUT #1 \ GOTO 10

100 IF X <> 0 THEN MOVE TO #1, FILL$ = (6-X) * 80% \ PUT #1
```

MOVE TO in line 50 of the above program dynamically allocates storage space in the I/O buffer. The FOR..NEXT loop (lines 10 to 60) assembles the records in the I/O buffer. Allocations are dynamic and can be changed in another line of the program. PUT in line 70 then writes the assembled block of data to disk.

Line 100 is used to FILL the buffer with spaces so that any data from an earlier operation will be deleted. If this were not done, there might at some point be confusion as to why duplicate data was in the file.

As was implied in the introduction to this chapter, most modern disk systems block and deblock data without program interference. Many applications programs can be written without concern for disk utilization. Yet, there are often instances when it is useful to PUT and GET blocks of data from within the program. The concept is similar to using relative files and can be of value in processing linked and inverted lists. BLOCK I/O simply puts the strength of the system in the progammer's hands.

X.D   REVIEW QUESTIONS

1. Explain how data can be blocked and deblocked. Who decides the blocking factor? How does the system impose restrictions?
2. How can FILL be used in MAP statements? How is it used to mask data stored in buffers?
3. Can space for both relative and BLOCK I/O records be statically as well as dynamically allocated? How does the process work? Would it be the same for each?

4. Give some possible applications in which linked lists might be processed using BLOCK I/O files. Under what conditions would BLOCK I/O not be the best choice?

5. How are BLOCK I/O files similar to relative files? How might they also be used in place of indexed files?

6. What parameters might be used in determining which type of file organization would be best for a given application? Make a list for each type, pro and con.

X.E EXERCISES

1. Using the example for dynamic buffering, chart and write a program to run in your system.

2. Write a second program to retrieve the records and print them sequentially.

3. The college telephone switchboard needs a "small" program to find local telephone numbers upon request. The operator has a CRT and should be able to enter a professor's, staff member's, or student's name and then have their phone number displayed on the terminal.

   Names and numbers are added at the beginning of the semester. Any additions during the semester are kept in a special list.

   BLOCK I/O files are to be used to store the data, using master blocks as diagrammed in the section on BLOCK I/O and indexed files.

   Several students can work on this project—one for each program. Again, be sure to agree on all formats before designing the programs. Also consider any special problems: for example, what happens if there are two Mary S. Jones, and the first ends a block and the second begins the next block?

   a. The first program should create the master blocks and store the data.

   b. The second program is used to update changes in phone numbers. Changes to names and additions are put in a special list.

   c. The third program is used by the operator for making inquiries.

Index